The Coaches' Motivational Playbook

Eddie Hill
Jim Moore

ISBN: 978-1-58518-022-6
Library of Congress Control Number: 2006940921

Book layout: Bean Creek Studio
Cover design: Melissa Monogue/Backporch Productions

Coaches Choice
P.O. Box 1828
Monterey, CA 93942
www.coacheschoice.com

Dedication

This book is dedicated to all coaches who lead, inspire, and change lives daily. You have our utmost respect and appreciation.

Acknowledgments

I would like to thank my parents for teaching me the importance of teamwork, and my wife and best friend for supporting me throughout this entire project.
—Eddie Hill

My contribution to this project has been a direct result from learning that in life wins are sweeter and losses not as bitter when shared with family and friends. Thanks to all of you who continue to motivate me.
—Jim Moore

We would also like to thank Ron and Alice Adams, who helped make this book possible, and Kim Iske, for her helpful edits. Lastly, we would like to thank all the staff at Coaches Choice, especially Dr. Jim Peterson.

Contents

- Coaching Today's Players: Generation Y
- How to Speak With and Coach Mr. and Ms. Indifferent
- Confidential Letter to Myself
- How to Motivate a Team with "The M.O.T.I.V.A.T.E. Method"

- Can You Learn Through a Clinched Fist? Maybe . . .
- Motivation from a Little Friend
- The Secret Society of the Gold Dot
- Crossing the Rubicon through Commitment
- The "Dumbbell Theory:" The Key Is Teamwork
- For All the Marbles
- A Valuable Lesson from a Potato and a Straw
- Lesson from a Lunchbox
- Burning the Ships: Motivated to Succeed
- Tipping the Scales
- Seeing the Light
- Tongue Depressors
- Flying the Victory Flag
- Four Difficult Motivation Situations

Introduction

The Coaches' Motivational Playbook is designed to help coaches answer the age-old question: "How can I get the most out of my players?" At one time or another, every coach has probably said to himself, "I know these are good players, but how can I elevate their play and help them reach their full potential?" This volume is the "how-to" book coaches have been looking for, filled with proven step-by-step methods on motivation from coaches and players at every competitive level. Initially, the book addresses the authors' observation that coaches should be able to motivate anyone—even those who seem to be indifferent. Being indifferent seems to be an attribute that many current players share. This book provides coaches with a strategy that works.

While theory is great, what coaches most often need is a road map from their coaching colleagues who have had success and can point out the shortcuts and barriers to avoid because many of them have traveled the same road many times. In an easy-to-understand and -apply manner, this book explains how coaches can motivate their players using the proven M.O.T.I.V.A.T.E. method, which is a systematic plan of action appropriate for every player.

Coaches will see immediate results from their efforts to motivate their players by setting realistic goals, using the Player Goal Sheet, as well as learning specific recognition techniques that work. Scientific and practical research shows that players will be more likely to give 100 percent effort if they know they are appreciated, and in this regard *The Coaches' Motivational Playbook* shows coaches how.

The book also includes a number of team motivational exercises and ideas that coaches from across the country have employed, as well as a list of team mottos that teams can adopt. How often have coaches sat and thought, "What can I say to my players to fire them up?" As such, the book offers actual speeches that can be adapted to a particular program, as well as pep rally talks and quotes. A section on how coaches can motivate the indifferent athlete is also presented.

Throughout the book, a "motivational vocabulary" is employed to assist coaches and players in their efforts to develop and apply different motivational talks and phrases that will mean something to their intended audiences. Not only do their players look to their coaches for motivation, but members of their community often do as well. More often than not, they routinely want to challenge and inspire these individuals. This book can help give coaches those words. All coaches need to do is simply add their own enthusiasm.

Another major factor that The *Coaches' Motivational Playbook* addresses is how to mold each group of players into a true team. The truth is coaches can achieve this goal, and when it happens, it is magical. The V.I.C.T.O.R.Y. system detailed in the book tells coaches how to transform individual effort into team success. Coaches will also find out how to make your practices more fun and how to have teambuilding events that can help bring their players together into a cohesive unit.

This book is called a "playbook" because it is filled with the X's and O's of how to motivate players and create a team. Like any good coaches playbook, plenty of options exist.

Read, enjoy, and have the greatest season ever.

How to Truly Motivate Others

Joe Robbins / Zuma Press

> Question: "How do you motivate other people?"
>
> Answer: "Give others what they want and need, and you will get what you want and need."
>
> —Steven Richards

Everyone is motivated by something. As a coach, it is your responsibility to figure out what that "something" is. Once you do, you will be amazed at what you can help your players accomplish. Somewhat surprisingly, doing so is not as hard as you might think.

As a coach, you have probably learned over the years that different teams are motivated by different factors. For some teams, the chief motivating factor could be winning a state championship. As such, they are motivated to do whatever it takes to win. Other teams may be sick of losing, which motivates them to strive to reach a winning record. Every team has at least one thing in common, however. Something is driving them to want more. That something is the "catalyst"—the idea, the object, the driving force behind what they do.

One of the underlying principles of this book is that the key to motivating anyone is: give others what they want and need and you will get what you want and need. As was mentioned previously, all you need to do is figure out what others want and need. *The Coaches Motivational Playbook* explains how. Once you are able to determine your team's catalyst (the reason why your players want to compete so hard), you are on your way. In response, you need to focus and build your program around the obtainable goals you have identified and develop a plan to hit those goals. Of course, coaches use all kinds of items and/or steps to help their team reach their goals—including programs, slogans, team-building exercises, rallies, and stickers on helmets, etc. This book is designed to provide you with many of the resources you will need to motivate your team. Regardless of your team's specific goal, always remember that the key to motivating any team is finding what the team wants and then focusing your resources and energy on achieving that goal.

What about individual players? How do you specifically motivate them? Again, remember the mantra: "Give others what they want and need and you will get what you want and need." Because all players are motivated by something, as their coach all you have to do is to determine what that particular motivating factor is. The key is to remember that four different factors drive most people:

- Results—often the team leader
- People—the goofy, light-hearted kid
- Security—quiet, steady player
- Quality—introverted, slow perfectionist

> The key to motivating anyone is: give others what they want and need and you will get what you want and need.
>
> All you need to do is figure out what they want and need, and *The Coaches' Motivational Playbook* will tell you how.

As such, each motivating factor lends itself to a distinctly different personality type. In this regard, all you need to do is figure out which type of "personality" each of your players is.

Age, position, family income, and race have no bearing into which of the four categories players fit. Intelligence or athletic ability also has no influence. Based on research conducted by renowned psychologist Dr. W.M. Marston, depending on their dominant nature, people usually can be classified into one of the four aforementioned categories. Of course, they may exhibit a few traits in other areas, but on the whole every player simply falls into one of the four categories. Furthermore, individuals don't usually shift from one category to another—in other words, they are who they are.

Gaining a better understanding of the four types of personalities and their attendant motivational characteristics can enable coaches to be better prepared to handle their athletes in an appropriate manner. In that regard, an overview description of each category and a list of guidelines/suggestions for dealing with individuals who would fall into a particular classification include the following:

Results Oriented

Results-oriented players are all about getting results now. These individuals need to get things done. They are often the leaders on the team who are giving the best effort. For example, a middle linebacker who is a results-oriented person simply wants to get the quarterback, and nothing will stop him. A setter in volleyball will almost kill herself getting to any ball, because her goal is to set up her teammates for the spike. The key point is that "results-oriented players" are aggressive in almost all areas of their lives. The following considerations can help you when you're dealing with this type of athlete.

- Consider thinking outside the box to find creative ways to push them. They will always be looking for new challenges, and you may help them find new avenues for their passion.

- Keep in mind that although very few players will fall in this category, those that do will be great examples for the rest of the team. Don't be surprised when they become frustrated with other members of the team who are not as aggressive as they are or willing to move as fast as they think they should.

- When you deal with them, be quick and to the point. Remember that they don't need a lot of details. Just give them the ball, and watch out. Don't expect them to be the most sensitive people in the world. As a rule, most individuals in this category are quite the opposite.
- Always keep in mind that a results-motivated player can be a huge asset to your team, both as an example and a leader.
- Among examples of high-profile, results-oriented athletes and coaches are: Tiger Woods, Michael Jordan, Bill Belichek, and Pat Summitt.

Soccer great Mia Hamm noted what it was like to be an athlete who was motivated by results: "You can't ever live with good enough. Sometimes, deciding to be the best feels great. Sometimes, it's discouraging. And almost always, it's exhausting. The bottom line is: if I don't go into it every day consistently committed, I won't get results." In a similar vein, Pat Summitt described her upbringing when she stated: "In my family, good work was expected, not praised. Excuses weren't accepted and laziness wasn't tolerated. I don't mind being tough because my dad was tough. I don't mind showing affection because my mother showed affection."

It may be helpful for you to note which players on your team are results-oriented, and what you can do to get the most out of these individuals. Keep in mind: these individuals may not be your best athletes. Rather, these athletes simply possess a *driving force* to get things done.

> Frankly, you don't have to motivate the results-type. Those players will go after their goals on their own, and they may even push you.

People Oriented

People-oriented players want to be liked by other people. These individuals are the really outspoken players on the team. They want to be noticed, respected, and rewarded. The traits that they tend to exhibit include:

- Talkative, funny, inspirational at times.
- Extremely optimistic, almost to a fault. However, when everyone else is down, they will still be smiling and encouraging their teammates.
- Sometimes frustrating to you, because they often will be the ones "playing around" when you need them to focus.
- Crave attention and have a need to be recognized.

As might be guessed, you can motivate them by recognizing them more often, speaking to them, and showing them more attention. Frequently, you will also have to help them focus on realistic goals. More often than not, they tend to think "more highly" of themselves and their abilities than circumstances would otherwise dictate. The following points can help you be better prepared to deal with people-oriented players:

- Character issues attendant to these athletes may be a problem. Because they so desperately want to please others, they sometimes make bad choices.
- Coaches who fall into this type might be great at recruiting, but are not as proficient at drawing up plays.
- People-oriented types also often lack follow-through and change plans quickly.
- Overall, however, people-oriented athletes can be positive driving forces that every team needs.
- To help motivate these players, it is important that you ask them for their opinion on critical issues.
- Allow these players to talk whenever possible—they love to be heard.
- Talk to these players more than others. They crave the attention and go to great lengths to please the coach and others.
- At times, you may need to take these players off to the side and let them know you need their help by paying more attention in meetings and practices, as well as setting a good example in all they do.
- Among examples of well-known people-oriented athletes and coaches are Chad Johnson, Deon Sanders, Michael Irvin, Muhammad Ali, Pat Riley, and Lou Holtz.

It may be helpful for you to note which players on your team are people-oriented players, and what you can do to get them to help your program. Keep in mind that because their attention-craving antics may be a distraction to the team, you'll need to get them to focus on more important matters.

Security Motivated

Security-motivated players can best be described as individuals who need security and stability. While these players may not be the most talented athletes, they work hard, steadily, and staunchly, day in and day out. The following observations can help you to be better prepared to deal with security-motivated players:

- This type of player is the backbone of any team, and can be described as a "worker bee."
- They are very quiet and seldom will be the captain of the team.
- They will show up for practice on time and do a good, solid job.
- As a general rule, they will not give their ideas on what will make the team better, but will reflect for attributes associated with being a steady, hard worker.

- Steady, security players do not like change and do not adapt very well to it.

- Because of their general sense of insecurity, you may have to explain changes to them and reasons for any planned changes. Once these athletes see the "big" picture, they will adapt slowly.

- They will not quit the team. They will stick through relatively difficult situations long past other personality types.

- To motivate the security-oriented person, you need to make sure they see how they fit into the big picture. While they will not get (nor will they seek) the limelight, they need to feel they are an integral part of the team and are appreciated. A lot of linemen in football fall into this category. They show up, do their jobs, and hope their name is not noticed—during or after the game.

- Although having them compete for their position on the team may cause them a substantial level of anxiety and stress, it may also push them to another level of performance.

- Among the more well-known examples of security-oriented athletes and coaches are: Tim Duncan, Annika Sorenstam, John Madden, Lovie Smith, and Joe Paterno.

It may be helpful for you to note who on your team is a steady player (and who is motivated by needing security) and what you can do to make these players feel important and a part of the big picture. Keep in mind that these players are the backbone of your team—both in deed and by example.

> "Lombardi was a friend of mine who motivated through fear. The Dallas Cowboys had a system: we taught players, that's how we motivated."
> —Tom Landry
>
> A system is a clear sign of motivation through a quality style.

Quality Oriented

Quality-oriented personalities are motivated by doing a quality job. On occasion, they may be slower to act, because they are thinking about their performance, but once they understand what is expected of them and how to fulfill those expectations, they do a very good job. The following observations can help you deal with quality-oriented athletes:

- Quality-oriented individuals will not settle for anything but near perfection. In the business world, they are engineers and accountants. In sports, they are the fans who are statisticians who know every statistic about your team. In athletics, they are players who are rarely satisfied—even with a good performance.

- They are usually very introverted, because they are thinking about a better way to do things. As a rule, they won't share their ideas unless you ask.

- In athletics, these types of athletes are consumed with the perfect pass route, the perfect golf swing, and so forth.

- One drawback that these types of individuals often face is that perfection takes time. You must give them time to get things right.

- Coaches will often be frustrated with people who are motivated by quality, because they want them to be something they are not. Even though they can throw a perfect spiral or have an excellent jump shot, they cannot lead others, except through their exemplary play. They are not vocal.

- To motivate these types of players, you should give them a task to do and let them do it. Show them the correct technique, and they will get it right.

- Be patient with them. They are thinking—and perfection usually takes time.

- Recognize their contribution and let them know that you appreciate their ideas.

- Examples of high-profile people who are motivated by quality include: Jerry Rice, Peyton Manning, LaDamian Tomlinson, and Tom Brady.

It may be helpful for you to note who on your team is a quality-driven individual. Keep in mind that even though they may not be vocal, you should try to determine how they can help the team become successful.

While all people are motivated by one of the previously mentioned four factors, one problem that many coaches encounter is determining what motivates those athletes who are indifferent or don't seem to care. On occasion, these players may have initially been excited about the season, but suddenly they don't seem to care. Make no mistake, however, they are still motivated by one of the four primary factors. In this situation, they temporarily fit into the category of "security." More than anything else, they want to be accepted by their friends. On the other hand, they still want to be part of the team. They crave being accepted by someone or some thing. Fortunately, the team can meet the player's needs, but it will take effort and understanding on the part of their coaches. It should be noted that greater detail on how to stimulate this type of player and how to keep him excited about the game is provided later in this chapter.

It should be emphasized that none of these types of athletes are any better than others—just different. If you take the time to get to know your players by talking to and observing them, it is amazing what you can learn. All factors considered, it comes back to our initial premise: if you give your athletes what they want and need, you will get what you want and need in return.

What is it that coaches want? Most coaches want to win and make a positive difference in the lives of their players. By definition, although most coaches are generally results-oriented, it is crucial that they understand not everyone shares their value system or places the importance on winning that they do. Individual players have a diverse array of needs and priorities. Amazingly, if you motivate your players by recognizing their individual needs, your team will be more successful as a result. In the process, everyone (you and your athletes) will benefit.

In our opinion, Lou Holtz was sadly mistaken when he said, "Motivation is simple. You eliminate those who are not motivated." In reality, we have never met a player who could not be motivated by the proper approach. The key point to remember is that in real life, everyone is motivated differently. As such, if you are willing to use the tools and information detailed in this book, you will enhance the likelihood that you will get what you want—championships and more importantly, champions.

Coaching Today's Players: Generation Y

Who are and what is generation Y? The answer to this question may help you address the issue of how you can motivate those individuals who seem to be disinterested. Certainly, not all kids fall into the category of being "indifferent." Helping you figure out what to do with those that do, however, is an essential focus of this chapter.

Generation Y is the generation of young people on your team. Generation Y—also referred to as the "echo," "net," or "why" generation—are those Americans who were born between 1978 and 1994. They are 60 million strong, second in number only to the baby-boomer population of 72 million. You have probably asked yourself, "Why are these players having fun on the bus after we just lost a game?" The answer may involve a myriad of factors. In reality, a number of factors have driven this generation to be vastly different from all previous generations, including:

- They are growing up with the Internet.
- They are also growing up with cell phones, text messaging, and instant messaging.
- They have always had video games to play—often one at home and one to carry with them.
- Unlike generations before them, they are often included in making family decisions. This scenario includes anything from what car to buy to what to have for dinner.
- Because of their substantial access to information, they are a relatively informed generation (when they want to be).
- This generation is often very socially tolerant.
- As a rule, they are very nonjudgmental.
- They are interactive.

- Three out of four individuals have working mothers.

- Nearly one of three births in the early 1990s was to an unmarried woman. With approximately one in three marriages ending in divorce, obviously a significant portion of this generation will spend at least part of their childhood in a single-parent home.

- Generation Y is also the first generation to experience a decline in overall sports participation, basically due to declining participation in traditional fitness-related activities.

- They are big on credibility (e.g., "street cred").

- They are lacking in accountability.

- They respond to humor, irony, and the truth.

- Although edgy (and at times anxiety-ridden), they tend to be optimistic about the future.

What does all this mean? It means this generation is marked by several traits, including:

- A low threshold for boredom

- Shorter attention spans than previous generations

- A preference for action over observation

Because of their access to computers, cell phones, instant messaging, and text messaging, this generation stays in constant contact with their friends. A technological connectedness exists amongst this generation like never before. Being connected to their peers is what drives much of what they do and in a sense defines who they are. Understanding this connectedness is monumental in understanding Generation Y. And, understanding this connectedness is even more than monumental in understanding why they choose to play organized sports.

Four Main Reasons Kids Play Sports

- To have fun

- To compete

- For social reasons

- To be on a team

Game day is important because it is fun. It's not about fitness or helping a coach get a better job. They play to laugh and have fun. The games are fun, the pep rallies are great, and the game itself is tremendous. The other parts, quoting them, "suck." While you must practice, sacrifice, and work hard, it is only a means to an end for them, which is to play better and to have more fun. In the program *Coaching to Change Lives*, a player recently summed it up for an excited coach who had just hit town and was talking about going to win this and win that. One player went to the coach and said, "You're not going to like it here. You're here to win, we are here to play."

Kids play games. They play in the sandbox. Later they play soccer and don't even keep score, and at the end of the season they get a ribbon for being on a team. They are encouraged, their self-esteem gets built up, and then all of a sudden all anyone cares about is their record. Make no mistake, winning is fun, but don't tell any parent that their child is any less special because they lost a game when a field-goal kicker missed wide right. Keep things in perspective. They call it a "game" for a reason. This book offers many suggestions to help you motivate your players. The best tip is simply to remember why they play in the first place.

Remember: give others what they want and need and you will get what you want and need. Kids play to have fun, to compete and to be on a team with their friends. If you work a little harder, you can make it more fun and you will win.

Dan Coryell found himself in a situation once before playing in the Rose Bowl with his team. He said they were nervous and would not relax. Finally, he said, "Fellows, we are going to play like fighting ducks today. That's right, ferocious fighting ducks. I want all of you to go into this huge stadium and quack like a duck." Everyone began laughing, ran out into the stadium quacking and were relaxed enough to win the game. Air Coryell was not afraid to lighten things up and it made the difference between winning and losing. We are not advocating being goofy; we are saying at times it may prove beneficial to lighten up. Then, when your team really does need to bear down, they will because the overall <u>total</u> experience is fun. If you want your players to play harder and to be focused, remember:

- For the results-type personality, achieving the goal is fun. Getting a trophy or ring makes it worth all the work, and they will work like crazy to achieve their goal.

- For the player that is motivated by people, they want to please others, including adults. They will work hard to please you if you have earned their respect.

- For the security-motivated player, they want to be a part of the team so bad they will work hard to keep their position.

- For those motivated by quality, use patience because it may take them more time to develop into a really good player.

It is important to keep score. As players graduate and enter the full-time workforce, they will find a world where everyone is accountable to someone. Bill Gates reminds us to hold players accountable, to teach them that life rewards those who put in the extra effort. Even though many from Generation Y seem to be uninterested in much going on with the team (especially any extra effort required), they do want to participate and enjoy winning. Players today are different than past generations, and they must be dealt with differently. In the past, coaches could say "Jump," and players would only ask, "how high?" If you ask today's player to jump, the response very well may be, "Why?"—which, if you think about it, is not a bad question.

For the indifferent player, keep it fun, keep it competitive, and give plenty of recognition. Also, make them realize how special it is to be part of a team. One coach said the numbers of kids playing high school football is down. I wonder why. All players need to understand that working hard is a part of being on a team and is an important part of success. How do you make the players understand it is important to be on your team? Try doing something special when they wear your logo for the first time. Don't just hand out jerseys. Make them earn it and make it a special occasion. If it means more, they will work harder to earn it.

> The good news is: if you keep the practices fun, and if you emphasize how important it is to be on a team and keep things competitive, your team will play hard and win!

> The reason they seem to be happy on the bus after a win or loss is they played the game and that was what they wanted to do. "Back in the day," coaches and players wanted to win. It may not be as important to many now.

How to Speak With and Coach Mr. and Ms. Indifferent

The key to dealing with this generation is talking to the players. This generation is not sold on authority, yet they respond to candor. Credibility is high on their list, so speak honestly. They will not respond to your frustration and using accusatory language will not move them.

- Do not attack them. Talk to them.
- Be specific on why you want them to do something. If you give them a reason, they will be more likely to perform.

Example #1

Coach: "Casey, let me tell you what I have observed lately. I have noticed you are the last one out of the locker room when practice starts and the first in the locker room when practice is over. On top of that, yesterday you seemed a bit distracted during practice."

Speak next in terms of the team. Explain how this behavior is affecting the team. Once again be careful not to go on the attack.

Example #2

Coach: "Casey I need everyone to be focused during practice and during the games. When you are not focused, it affects the whole team."

At this stage, always remind the player how important he is to the team—whether he is a starter or not. Ask what he thinks about what you have said. Doing so will include the player in the conversation, which goes a long way with this generation.

Example #3

Coach: "Casey, do you agree with what I have said? Does what I am saying make sense? What do you think about what I am observing?"

(If they don't respond, you have at least shown respect, which is important to them.)

Develop a plan to change the behavior that includes them.

Example #4

Coach: "Casey, what do you think we should do differently?"

Generation Y responds well to being included in decision-making. You do not have to let them make the final decision, but allowing their input will build trust and credibility. The University of Tennessee won the NCAA women's basketball championship in 2007. One reason for their success is Coach Pat Summit's willingness to grow and change in her approach to coaching. Coach Summit has even been known to solicit players' opinions during time-outs. Too many coaches seem to think it is a sign of weakness to ask players anything. Keep in mind: Generation Y is different and must be coached differently to get better results.

Remember, if you want to get through to them and if you want to motivate them, you must remember why they play in the first place:

- Fun
- Friends
- Competition
- Team/belonging

Are these needs being met?

- Does he have friends on the team?
- Is he getting the opportunity to compete?

Agree to a plan of action and have the player make a commitment to the coach on how her/his behavior will be different. Teenagers, in general, are lacking when it comes to accountability.

Many coaches may feel they don't want to talk to players or use the ideas included. They may want to return to the old days where they could get away with saying, "It's my way or the highway." Those days are likely gone. Players today are different. Many do not and will not respond to this old-school approach. It does not mean they don't respect leaders and leadership because they do want to be part of a team. One coach summed it up simply and profoundly when he said: "I want to coach, just as if my son were on the team—with respect, direction, and care."

Your Ace in the Hole: Self-Written Confidential Letter for Players

As a coach, you may want to try one more thing with the player who has lost his motivation. *Before the season starts* when everyone on the team is still excited about the upcoming season, have them fill out a letter to themselves (Figure 1-1). This letter is totally confidential. Get all the players to fill one out and have them place their letter in an envelope. Have them seal it up and self address it. Later in the season when you feel a player needs some encouragement, pull out their letter and simply mail it. In their own words, they pledge not to quit and many other important agreements and thoughts. If your words don't ring the bell anymore, then maybe their own words will. You can mail all these at the same time after a tough loss or before a big game. No matter what, it will have an effect.

How to Motivate a Team With "The M.O.T.I.V.A.T.E. Method"

This book is entitled *The Coaches' Motivational Playbook* because the authors believe coaches need more than just a quote or loud voice to pump up individual players and the entire team. Each coach has his favorite play, but you can't run it all the time and succeed. Coaches realize to get the most out of players, they must have a plan, a series of ideas they can use to motivate their team. As you have learned, each person is unique and demands different motivational methods.

Following is a plan of action. For this step-by-step method for motivating players, these steps are interchangeable. To be really successful, make sure you use each step

Confidential Letter to Myself

(Each player will fill out and place in a self-addressed envelope.)

As I write this, I am very _____ about the team.

I have prepared for this year by _____ and _____.
I have sacrificed spending time _____ with (or doing)
_____ to excel. My personal goals for the season
are _____, _____ and _____.
To reach these goals I will _____ , _____ and
_____.

Some things that might stand in my way are _____ and
_____. I will try to control them, knowing my performance and the
team will suffer if I allow distractions.

I would like to give my all for _____,
_____ and _____. My motivation to
succeed comes from _____. My favorite thing
about the team is _____.

The word "quit" is not in my vocabulary. I will finish what I start, realizing even
though things may not always go perfectly for me—such is life, and I need to fight
through any adversity. This refusal to give up will prepare me for the rest of my life
and future trials. When things get tough, I will _____
_____. One good thing I expect to enjoy from this year is
_____.

The goals I have for the team are _____ and _____.

To help achieve this, I will _____ and _____.

A person on this team that I can help to achieve her goals and ultimately our team
goals is _____. If I _____, I will help her achieve
her goals which, in turn, will help everyone.

I recognize that it is an honor to be on the team and I am reminded, for whatever
reasons, many others cannot. I will do my best, grow from this experience and
learn lessons to last the rest of my life.

Sincerely,

_____

Figure 1-1. Confidential letter to myself

with all your players. Keep in mind, each team, like the players, has its own personality. These steps can be and should be used with the collective group.

- **M:** Meeting the players
- **O:** Obtainable goals
- **T:** Togetherness
- **I:** Inspiration
- **V:** Victory
- **A:** Accolades
- **T:** Talk and communication
- **E:** Enthusiasm

M—Meeting the Players

Meet the players and coaches. Really get to know your players. Every player is different. Ask any parent and they will tell you each child is "special" in their own way and needs different things. Some kids have very "thin skin," and when you yell they will ball up and quit. It may be that they come from an abusive home, and one ill-placed outburst from you causes memories to come out, pushing them over the edge—or off the team. Be especially careful not to yell at the fun-loving, people-motivated player. He will be embarrassed and may respond in inappropriate ways.

It is important to get to know the kids. Who are their parents or who else will be sitting in the stands, rooting them on, and what are their future goals? If you don't have time to gather this and other information, you are probably in the wrong profession because to build character and mold young people, you must know who you are working with. As Bear Bryant reminds us, "The biggest mistake coaches make is taking borderline cases and trying to save them. I'm not talking about grades; I'm talking about character. I want to know, before a boy enrolls, about his home life and what his parents want him to be." Every player is unique, and to truly motivate him, you must understand him. This book includes a player-personality profile for each player to fill out when the season starts. This profile will go a long way in helping you know your team. Of course, the best way to get to know the players is simply talking with them. As a player, do you remember what a big deal it was when a coach talked to you? The same goes today. Players look up to their coaches and seek their approval. A little encouragement goes a long way!

One coach from South Texas said he made home visits to meet the player's family and to learn more. At first, it was to verify where the players actually lived where they said they did. Later, the coaches realized the benefits of learning so much more about the young men. Parents and other family members had an entirely different outlook on the coach and program after that.

O—Obtainable Goals

Make sure your goals are written and achievable. You may think your athlete knows what you want of them, but be sure by writing down the goals and both agreeing to them. Also, make sure you have realistic goals the athlete can achieve. First, make smaller goals for the athlete, so they can find some success. Then they will be ready to move on. Zig Ziglar encourages people to break their long-range goals into two increments. Examples: If you want the student-athlete to run the 40-yard dash in 4.4 seconds, try shooting for 4.6 in the first 30 days and the next month 4.5. This approach is "doable" to the athlete and he won't give up. If you want an athlete to bench press 250 pounds, start with a smaller, achievable weight and watch him progress. This important topic will be covered in more detail in Chapter 3.

T—Togetherness

On a team, you have the luxury of not having to make every decision or handle every motivating situation. If cultivated and trained, leaders will step up to these challenges. Again, give assistants and student leaders opportunities where they can excel. If you expect an assistant coach or a player to step up, he will. People usually meet our expectations. Cultivate working together. Bear Bryant said, "I don't hire anybody not brighter than I am. If they're not smarter than me, I don't need them." What did Coach Bryant know? The staff was smarter than the individual. Use the gifts and talents of those around you.

Also, have senior players talk to younger players. Consider making "inner squads" with groups of eight or so players. Younger players can be overwhelmed by huge teams, and these smaller groups can benefit the entire team. Players step up and other players learn from their example. This approach is significantly different than just placing them together by positions. Together these smaller "family" groups help meet a lot of needs. After all, you are all in this together. Another great idea adopted by so many teams is to have a buddy or mentor system where a senior gets paired up with a freshman to help the freshman get along better during the season. This program will really help ensure the player surrounds himself with quality people.

> "The real secret to winning football games is to work more as a team, and think team first and less about the individual. I play not my eleven best but my best eleven that think as one."
>
> —Knute Rockne

I—Inspiration

Tell the players why you are challenging them. Let them see your vision and how everyone will benefit. Players in the generation today need to know why. It is not enough anymore to say, "Because I said." Players will follow if they feel you have their best interest in mind and have a plan.

Ways to Inspire People:

- Set a good example. If you show you have a genuine interest, players will listen. (Included in this playbook is a section on showing that you care. Check it out for suggestions. You may find some things you could incorporate.) If you are on time, they will be on time. Show that you respect their time and they will do the same.

- Have a positive attitude. People want to hear a positive good message and will be inspired if they do. Be mindful of the things you say and do; players and coaches are watching. What does your body language show? What are you really projecting? To be inspiring does not mean you need eloquent words or speeches. It means to lift others up, which can be accomplished in many ways. If you do inspire, watch out because the victories will come.

V—Victory

Student-athletes play to have fun, but winning is fun. Victory means different things to different people. Victory may mean being on a team for the very first time and starting to see beyond themselves to others who matter. Victories may mean meeting new friends with healthy values and morals and leaving others behind who don't have your best interest in mind. Victory may mean growing physically and starting to see muscles bulging that players didn't even know they had. Victory could be becoming a starter for the first time and feeling so proud.

Young people grow and change so much faster than adults. They are not limited by a lifetime of negativity, and they want to please others and make them proud. Today, many student-athletes have coaches who will help them graduate, and they will be the first in their family to go to college. This situation is a victory for everyone. With a little motivation, you can give victory to an entire family and not even know it.

> "Coaches who can outline on a blackboard are a dime a dozen. The ones *who win* get inside their players and motivate."
>
> —Vince Lombardi

A—Accolades

The truth is that all of us like to be recognized. People want to be recognized for their efforts, and it seems the more you lift them up, the more they want to achieve. It doesn't always have to be a big ceremony or plaque on the wall. Sometimes just a simple pat on the back or "atta-boy" works fine. Accolades mean you have been noticed. When you give recognition to someone, make it specific. If you are telling the team they did a good job today, tell them what they did right. To get better quality, reinforce the positive. "Hey, guys! Great job on hitting those patterns perfectly." "Hey, ladies, those passes are crisp and hit the player perfectly, good job!" Next practice, you won't even have to mention it and can go onto another area that needs work. Business has learned this lesson well. In the old days, top salespeople could expect cash bonuses. What management and sociologist found out in most cases is that showing appreciation instead of just giving money brought greater results. What can you do to honor those who really work hard? Game balls are great, but how about practice balls or $2.00 medals. It's not the amount you spend, but the idea that you spent your time remembering them.

Richard Du Bois

T—Talk and Communication

Every good team communicates effectively. Any marriage and successful organization realizes that to be effective, you must share information. To develop a successful game plan, get the input of others. Regularly-scheduled opportunities will make it easier for everyone to know when the best time is to share their knowledge. Not asking people for their ideas is like owning a small lake with no fresh water supply coming in. It wouldn't be long before you have a dying, stagnant mess on your hands. One of the highest compliments you can pay people is to seek their opinions. This statement will prove to be true with both players and coaches. Communicate with them and include them, and you will get the most out of them.

A speaker one Sunday in church said, just before taking up the offering, "I have good news and bad news. We have all the money we need to pay our bills. We can pay the preacher, the light bill, and everything. The bad news is, it's still in your pockets." Teams have everything they need to be successful if they would just dig inside, work together, and communicate.

E—Enthusiasm

The last piece of the motivation plan is to be enthusiastic. Everyone is watching what you do and say, and they want to follow positive leaders. Smiling is the best way to be enthusiastic. People like it and will want a piece of what you have. Enthusiasm is the fuel that keeps the dream alive. Be enthusiastic and watch how others respond. Among the many ways to motivate others, a positive attitude and enthusiastic spirit is the best.

Enthusiasm is the secret ingredient of success for the most successful people as well as the generator of happiness. Norman Vincent Peale summed it up: "What goes in the mind is what determines the outcome. When an individual really gets enthusiasm, you can see it in the flash in their eyes, in the alert and vibrant personality. You can see it in the verve of the whole being. Enthusiasm makes the difference in one's attitudes toward other people, toward one's job, toward the world."

2

Motivational Exercises and
Object Lessons

Albert Dickson / Zuma Press

A key to motivating any team is to keep things fresh and challenging. Coaches are always looking for an edge, a way to pump up their players, or to teach the importance of a particular subject. The best way to teach someone is by demonstrating through the use of objects or events, anything visual. Players simply don't hear everything you are saying, but they will learn and pay attention if you do something to help make your point.

> "Remember, when you hear something, you forget it.
>
> When you see something, you remember it.
>
> But not until you do something will you understand it."
>
> —Chinese proverb

Can You Learn Through a Clinched Fist? Maybe ...

Coach Iske at Grapeland, Texas, recently told of an impromptu exchange with his players when trying to get the offensive line to understand the importance of teamwork. He said he simply called all the players together and said, "Jones, come up here." (Jones was the biggest lineman on the team.) "Jones, if I took my open hand like this and slapped you across the face would it hurt?" Jones replied, "Well, yeah coach. It would hurt." All the players began to laugh but were watching very intently. The coach continued, "Jones, would that slap knock you out or send you to the hospital?" Jones said, "No, coach. It would hurt, but I don't think it would cause that much damage." The coach then held his hand high in the air for all the players to see and asked, "What if I took my open hand and simply began folding in my fingers one at a time and slowly made it into a fist? Jones, do you think that would really hurt and cause some damage?" "Yeah," said the player. "That would hurt, and no telling what it would do?" The coach then asked the player to sit down. The coach addressed the team, "That's what I am talking about, men. You know a slap wouldn't do much to Jones—although I don't recommend even trying it. Jones is tough, but a fist might do some damage. Individual fingers on a hand are frankly weak, but together, once made into a tight tool, it is quite a force to reckon with. If we tighten up and work together, we can strike a mighty blow as well. What is it going to be, men? Can we work together and become really strong?"

What objects or ideas can you use to make a point for your team? Be creative. You don't have to say a lot to make a simple, yet powerful, point. Grant Teaff, the former head football coach of the Baylor University football program (and eventual athletic director for the school), said, "Motivation is simply a force, tangible or intangible (sometimes both), that propels someone to action. It is the most vital part of human life. Ultimately, that is the key to all success." The exercises described in this chapter can propel a team into action and make a point to last a season and beyond. Once they are in your brain, you will never forget them.

Motivation From a Little Friend

One of the most famous motivational ideas came from Coach Teaff back in 1978 as he was preparing his Baylor Bears for a game against the University of Texas. Teaff explains that while Baylor had a great season, they had tough losses to several powerhouse teams, which left the team "fragile and could cause them to come into the game against Texas tight and tense." He wanted the players to understand that the team would need exceptional individual effort to win, and that the difference between winning or losing would be individuals making big plays—maybe even "distasteful and painful plays requiring sacrifice."

Teaff was reminded of a story he had heard and decided to tell about how two Eskimos who were fishing out on the ice. Both cut the exact same hole and used the exact same bait. One fisherman was catching fish, while the other was not. Finally, one fisherman looked at the other and said, "You are catching fish and I am not. What is the secret to your success? The fish-catching fisherman looked the other man in the eye and said, "You gotta keep the worms warm."

As Teaff uttered those words, he stuck his tongue behind the bottom part of his lip to show the players where the fisherman kept his worms, in his mouth. Warm, wiggly worms will catch more fish than frozen worms. A distasteful job? Yes, but one that created success. The players got the point. One has to do whatever it takes to get the job done.

Later, Teaff consulted with a senior player and told him of his plan to "finish" the story with his players on Saturday just before the big game. The player enthusiastically encouraged him to go forward. Before the pre-game warm-up in the locker room, Coach Teaff gathered his players and reminded them of the story he had first told them three days earlier about the importance of "keeping your worms warm" to remind them of the incredible effort that would be needed to win and to plant the seed for what was to come.

Seconds before the game, Teaff gathered the troops again and said, "I have never seen a team work harder. Now, it is up to you. There is little the coaches can now do. But for me, while you are winning the game, I'm willing to keep the worms warm." With that, he pulled out a little friend from his pocket, held him high in the air, cocked open his lower jaw, and dropped him into the corner of his mouth. The players went nuts and rushed onto the field, laughing and loose. They went on to reach their goal—beating Texas 38-14.

The Secret Society of the Gold Dot

Before the 1979 spring football season, Grant Teaff decided to motivate his team by giving them a little reminder of their goals for the upcoming season. His outstanding book, *Grant Teaff with the Master Coaches*, tells the story of when he took a hole punch and made small gold dots out of helmet tape. He invited his players over to his home by class and each player come forward in his den. He then placed a dot on the player's watch over the six, or in their wallet if they weren't wearing a watch.

The coach then went on to explain, "These dots are gold to remind you of the Baylor University colors and they are meant to remind you of the goals you have set for this season." He then told them not to tell anyone what the dots meant, which he went on to explain:

- "G stands for the goals that you have set. You'll be reminded that your goals are to have a winning season and to get to play in a bowl game. To reach those goals, you must work hard and be prepared at all times.

- "O stands for the oneness it takes to be successful as a team. A major team goal for their team the year before was unity, and when faced with adversity they stuck together—which made them stronger. Oneness, stick together, and remember the team.

- "L stands for loyalty. Loyalty is the foundation on which to build success. Loyalty means you may not agree with everything, but you will commit yourself totally. Being a loyal person means you will stand up for your teammates, your coaches, your school, and (most important) yourself.

- "D stands for determination. Determination signifies that you, as an individual, will commit to completing a project. You are going to do whatever it takes to get the job done. Be determined that you will be in the best shape of your life, your outlook will be positive, and you will have a winning attitude."

He reminded them to tell no one, and later in the week he invited the other players and coaches to be initiated into the secret society. When the players returned in August for practice, they were met in the locker room with a green flag with a huge gold dot in the middle handing on the wall. It would be a daily reminder of their commitment to the 1979 season. That commitment became the foundation for Baylor's program that year as they went on to have a winning season and beat Clemson in the Peach Bowl. The next year, they won the Southwest Conference championship by three games.

Crossing the Rubicon Through Commitment

If you remember high school history, at some point you studied Julius Caesar. As you may remember, Julius Caesar was a great Roman General, very popular with his army and with the common folks. Those in the Roman Senate were becoming more concerned. Caesar was getting too popular and, thus, too powerful. So one day, as history tells us, Caesar was out admiring a country he had recently conquered when a runner came from Rome, saying the Senate wanted a word with him. More specifically, the Senate wanted Caesar to return to Rome immediately—but not with his army.

"Caesar, come home. Just make sure you come alone, so do not bring your army." Caesar was a smart man and suspected something was wrong. Could it be the Senate wanted to arrest him or, worse, to kill him? Coming to the Rubicon River, Caesar stopped. Why? An ancient law forbade any general from crossing the Rubicon River and entering Italy with his army. To do so was treason. So as Caesar stood on the banks of the Rubicon River, he had to make a decision. Should Caesar cross with his army or not? If he crossed over without his army, he would be taking a big risk. His friends back at the Senate could harm him—or not. If he crossed over the river with his army, there would be no turning back. He would be committing treason. "If I cross this river with my army, things will never be the same," he must have said to himself.

After several moments, Caesar decided to cross the river with his army, and the rest is history. The Roman leader who tried to trick Caesar fled to Greece and was killed by an ally of Julius Caesar. Caesar went on to become emperor of the most powerful empire in the world because he took his army who made a commitment to him and did not turn back. Big decisions wouldn't be big if they didn't have life-changing implications.

Application: Find a stream or creek. If you have to drive your team somewhere, the exercise is even more effective. Don't tell them where you are taking them. Just load them on a bus and go find a creek away from distractions. Once you arrive at the specific place:

- Speak briefly with your team about commitment.
- Speak with them about what it will take to reach their potential and about what it will take to become a team.
- Talk to them about long practices and discipline and sacrifice. Talk to them about always putting the team first. Then tell them the story of Caesar crossing the Rubicon River.

After the Story: Coaches can say, "We, as coaches, have made a big decision. We've made a life-changing decision. We've decided to work harder than we have ever worked before. Just like Caesar, we are solidifying that decision by crossing this stream. And like the decision Caesar made, once we cross over this 'river,' there will be no turning back. It will be tough, but we have decided."

Coaches then cross over. Once on the other side, you can tell your players, "To cross over this river is a big decision. We want all of you now to decide whether to cross or not to cross. If you choose to cross over:

- You are committing yourself to this team.
- You are making the decision to work as hard as you can and to give all that you can.
- You are dedicating yourself to always giving 110 percent.
- You are helping yourself and the team become champions.

"But know this. Once you cross over, there will be no turning back. We are going to work you hard, so hard that you may want to quit. But once you choose to cross, there will be no quitting. To cross over is a big decision. If you, in your heart, can make that decision, then come join us on the other side. For every step it takes to cross over is one step closer to becoming a champion."

Motto ideas using this theme:

- We decided.
- We crossed at the Rubicon.
- We crossed over.

The "Dumbbell Theory:" The Key is Teamwork

What Can a Dumbbell Teach You About Teamwork?

Materials Needed: Have two exact same dumbbells or weights for a group of five players.

- You can have as many groups as needed. Simply make sure the dumbbells or weights are somewhat heavy (five to seven pounds).
- Have your group in a circle. This exercise can be done in a locker room, gym, or wherever.
- It can also be done at a banquet, but substitute the weights with heavy glasses filled with water that are placed in the center of tables. These will look like centerpieces, but really they are for your object lesson.
- As the leader, tell the group to get in circles of no more than six players around the dumbbells placed on the ground or on a small table.
- Ask one person to pick up both dumbbells with one in each hand. Then, let him know not to change hands. (Again, don't make the dumbbell too heavy or too light.)
- Ask that person, "How much do you think the dumbbells weigh?"

- Let him answer. Don't be in a hurry. You want the dumbbells to start getting heavier. If it is a large group, don't ask individually. It will take too long.

- Ask, "Would you say the dumbbells weigh the same or different?" He will answer, "The same." (You can make a quick joke at this point everyone knowing the numbers are on the end of the dumbbells.)

- Tell the person holding the dumbbells to pass one around the circle while holding the other in the same hand. Remind them not to switch hands.

- As soon as they begin passing the other dumbbell from person to person in the circle, say, "Now, the dumbbell you are passing around represents all the work and goals we have for our team." (Go slowly. You want the one person to start struggling with the dumbbell.)

- Now say, "The dumbbell represents the struggles we will face and the victories we will enjoy." (Make sure the dumbbell goes around at least once if not twice. People may begin giggling, watching the one person struggle.)

- Then say, "Now, please pass the dumbbell back to the original person." (By this point, he will be worn out. Remind the person holding the dumbbells not to switch hands.)

- Say, "Now, tell me: which dumbbell feels like it weighs more, even though you know it is the same?" He will answer and you will respond, "Right! The one you have been holding on your own."

The point is that when you share the load as you did when you passed the one dumbbell, it didn't feel like it weighed anything. But when one person tries to carry the load, they struggle and have a difficult time. It really is true that many hands make for light work. Continue to share the load as a team and help each other out. (This approach works especially well when a team has a star player they are relying on too much.)

For All the Marbles

Purpose: "For All the Marbles" is a term whose origin is lost in history. Some historians think the phrase originated in ancient Rome where gambling on marble games was prevalent. In recent years, the term refers to the winning shot in a game of marbles, when the loser had to relinquish all of their marbles to the victor.

"For All the Marbles" can also be a team activity, used to motivate a team over a long period of time by filling a glass container full of marbles, which are deposited by the players on a designated time schedule. As the glass container begins to fill, it becomes a visual indicator to each person or the team of the progress they are making toward achieving their goals for the season.

Note: This activity is a motivational tool to be used over a long period of time, as opposed to an activity used for one game or one single event.

Set-Up: You will need a large, transparent container (clear glass, plastic or Plexiglas—a strong fish tank would work well) and a large sack containing enough marbles for the whole team to use for the entire season. (Fill the container with marbles to determine how many you will need.)

Description: On a time schedule determined by the coach, each player who believes he has achieved a stated goal or made a significant contribution during practice or during a game gets to deposit a marble in the large glass container. Coaches could also put extra marbles in when they feel the player has gone above and beyond in his effort. The collection of marbles signifies that the team—as a whole—is achieving the goals they set for the current season. Some teams may want to adopt "For all the marbles" as their team motto or slogan. A line needs to be drawn at the top of the jar.

Implementation:

- To develop interest in the activity, display the empty glass container with a poster stating, "What is this? Come see the Lions at their first game and find out." The container and poster could be displayed in such sites as various stores and restaurants in the community, the weight room during off-season, booster-club meetings, a trophy case in the school, and at pep rallies.

- Setting Goals: Coaches should be involved in guiding the team in setting their individual goals. Why? Because the first thing a player is going to say is, "My goal is to win District." If the team loses their first district game, the activity is no longer meaningful. Therefore, goals should be tied to each individual's performance over a period of time, such as a workout, a series of workouts, or a game.

- To develop player interest in "For All the Marbles," all coaches should refer to the activity during workouts. When giving instructions to the players, coaches should mention achieving team and individual goals. Players can be given a marble to carry around with them all the time. And coaches always have the option of giving or taking away marbles throughout the season—depending on effort. Players may have to walk around with two marbles in their pockets if they have given poor effort during that week. Two marbles will make a clicking sound as a constant reminder of the effort needed to succeed (and to get rid of the marbles and that sound).

A Valuable Lesson From a Potato and a Straw

If your team is struggling, try this motivational exercise using an unbaked potato and a straw. Like any magic trick, once you know the secret, the impact is over. However, before you show how the trick is done, you will be able to show everyone that attitude is everything. Before using this approach, practice first in private.

Set-Up: You will need a fresh, unbaked potato and a drinking straw (not one with a flexible portion in the middle). The challenge is to take the straw and push it through the potato. It will be very difficult. The straw will bend and people become frustrated very quickly.

The Solution: Simply place your thumb on the end of the straw, covering the air hole. Now when you try and push the straw through the potato, it will be much easier. As a matter of fact, if you practice this a few times, you will be amazed how well you can push the straw through.

The Teaching Moment

- Gather your players and tell them you want to talk about attitude and getting things done.
- "You know, team, when you think positively, it is amazing what you can do."
- "Take a potato, like this for instance, and a straw." (You can pass out a bunch of potatoes and straws for everyone or simply call on three or four people. Some will be able do to it, even if you don't tell them the secret, and that's okay.)
- "I want to see if you can stick the straw into the potato and push it all the way through."
- "Give it a try. How are you doing?" (Some will jab it in, others will slowly turn the straw). Mainly, they will struggle. Say, "Great job" to the ones who are able to do it, and invite them to sit down quickly.
- To the ones struggling, ask them, "Do you think you can get the straw through the potato?" Most will say, "No."
- Then tell them, "If you think you can, you probably can. If you think you can't, you won't."
- Next say, "Allow me to show you what I mean."
- Take the potato from someone who is struggling. Place your thumb over the open hole and while keeping the straw straight, jab it in. Do two in a row for effect if you like.
- At that point (and with a new straw) let them try again, and with confidence, they will be successful. We all have goals. Our particular goal is _____. If you think you can, you will; if you don't think you can, you can't. Make it happen with confidence.

> "If you think you can, you can.
>
> If you think you can't, you won't."

Lesson From a Lunchbox

Going to Work for a Winning Season

One inventive coach began the new season for his basketball team by issuing lunchboxes in the school colors. Nothing was inside the boxes except for a thermos bottle and a commitment contract for each player to sign, stating they were ready to go to work on the coming season and would settle for nothing less than hard work and committed effort to make this season the best ever.

The coach instructed his team, "For years, men and women have carried lunchboxes to the job site. Maybe some of your grandparents, parents, aunts, or uncles have done the same thing. The reason they took their lunchboxes was so that they could quickly have lunch and then get right back to work. For more generations than we represent here, the lunchbox has been a symbol—a symbol of the working men and women who reported to the factory or construction site or office every day to put in a full day's work.

"For our team, these lunchboxes represent that same tradition of hard work and commitment to our goals this season. I want you to carry these lunch boxes with you every day as a reminder of our total commitment to hard work, team effort, and getting the job done. From time to time coaches can add all kinds of motivating items to the player's lunch boxes. They can give the item directly to the player during practice or surprise the players by secretly adding items or messages.

"We'll expect to see these lunchboxes at every practice, every scrimmage, every pep rally, and every game. Every time you carry them, they are going to add to your load of books and workout gear, so it won't be easy. But these lunchboxes will continue to remind you and your teammates of your commitment to hard work and making this season the best yet.

"Before we end today, I want each of you to read and sign the commitment contract inside your lunchbox and have one of your coaches sign it as well before you put it back in the lunchbox. If, at any time during this season, you lose sight of our goals or what you're working so hard to achieve, I want you to open your lunchbox and reread your commitment. If you want to talk about it, I'll be available to discuss it with you at any time.

"So let's keep our focus on our goals by carrying our lunchboxes … our commitment to work hard, achieving our goals and making this season one that none of us will forget. Thanks, and Go _____!"

Burning the Ships: Motivated to Succeed

Historians have debated the authenticity of this story, however it is too good to ignore. In 1519, Spanish explorer Hernando Cortez had a plan to lead an expedition into Mexico. The plan was to go to Mexico to harvest its many treasures. The governor of Spain was so excited about the expedition that he granted Cortez a fleet of 11 ships and 700 men. The lands were fairly unknown for Cortez and his men. Legend has it that once they arrived in Mexico, Cortez had the men unload the ships and then Cortez gave the order for the ships to be burned. As they headed into their new adventure, the men turned back and saw all 11 ships burning.

Cortez did not know for sure what he and his men would encounter on this mission, but whatever it was, he did not want his men thinking that retreating was even a possibility. The option of going back had been eliminated. They were committed to success.

> "We will either find a way, or make one."
>
> —Hannibal

Tipping the Scales

The year was 1995. Gary Barnett was the head football coach at Northwestern University. Northwestern has always had a stellar reputation as an academic institution—but not as a football stalwart. They had not won a conference football championship or even played in a bowl game since the 1947 season.

Northwestern was opening the 1995 season against Notre Dame. Northwestern had not won a season opener since 1975 and was a 28-point underdog playing at Notre Dame, who had not lost a season opener since 1986.

With the season opener three weeks away, Coach Gary Barnett brought out a balancing scale. He alluded to the fact that Notre Dame had 19 practices until the season opener, and that they too had 19 practices. With that, he put 19 pennies on the Notre Dame side of the scale. On the Northwestern side of the scale, he put nothing. However, each day at the conclusion of practice, if the team had practiced hard, he would put a penny on the Northwestern side. Sure enough the scale—slowly, but surely—began to balance with each practice. Following is Gary Barnett's account of what happened, as told in his book *High Hopes*:

> We met as a team before we left for the stadium in the morning. I got out scales and put 19 pennies on each side. It was balanced. "We assume Notre Dame did everything it could," I said, "and we've earned

our 19." Then I took out a penny Jeff Genyk found (at the last practice at Notre Dame Stadium), and I said, "But we practiced the Sunday before we left for Kenosha, and that was actually one more time than they did." I put that penny on our side, and the scales tilted to us.

Then I said, "I do not want you to carry me off the field after this game. I want you to act like you've been here before, like you've done this before and you're used to this."

Northwestern went on to defeat Notre Dame 17–15 in what is now deemed by many as the biggest game in Northwestern football history. Northwestern used that season opening victory to springboard to their first conference championship and Rose Bowl birth in 48 years.

Seeing the Light

Materials Needed: A dark room, one penlight for each player, and a chair for each player

Description: This exercise was adapted from one shared by Gunter Brewer, receivers coach at Oklahoma State University. The coaches will have the players gather outside the dark room. Give each of the players a penlight. Instruct them not to turn the light on as they go in and find a chair in the dark room. The room needs to be pitch black. The players will need to sit in silence. The coaching staff speaks.

"Smith, can you see? Can you see the light?" (The starting quarterback works well since he often gets most of the publicity for the team.)

"No, coach."

"Smith, and only Smith, turn your light on." Smith turns on his light.

"Smith, do you think you have enough light now to find one of your receivers and complete a pass?" Smith will say, "No." The coach then says to the offensive line, "Offensive line, turn on your lights." They each turn on their lights, and the coach continues.

"Offensive line, can you see well enough to protect your quarterback? Can you even see well enough to get up and do some blocking drills?" If the room is dark enough, they will answer, "No."

The coach then says to the defensive line, "Defensive line, turn on your lights." They all turn on their lights and the coach continues. "Defensive line, can you see well enough to get up in this room and go through some drills?"

Then the coach asks the rest of the offense and then the rest of the defensive. When all the lights are on the coach speaks. "Team, can you now see the light? Can you see what happens when we all come together? Can you see how we need each other? It will take all of us, working together to achieve our goals. One light won't do it. Two lights won't do it. Three lights won't do it. Just the offensive line won't do it. Just the defensive line won't do it. But all of us together, we can do it."

Tongue Depressors

Materials Needed: Several tongue depressors

Description: This exercise is a tried-and-true demonstration about how teams are stronger when they work together. Give a player a tongue depressor and ask him to break it. He will be able to do so with great ease. Now, give him two tongue depressors. Holding them together, ask him to break them. He will be able to do so with relative ease. Next give him five. By the time you get to 10 or 11, even the strongest player will not be able to break them. Individually we are weak, but together we are unbreakable. It takes all of us working together to make a strong team.

Flying the Victory Flag

This technique is an excellent object lesson for teams who have been struggling to win for a long time or for a team trying to turn around a season. Coach Ron Adams tells of how one of his favorite uncles, who had been a Marine during World War II, told him about many of the terrible battles in which he had fought. As he told Ron about those battles, his fertile 10-year-old mind pictured his uncle planting the United States flag on Mount Suribachi during the Battle of Iwo Jima, just as he had seen on a poster.

I've thought about that image many times during my playing days. When things got tough in a game and my lungs were burning and my legs felt like rubber, I thought about putting up a flag with an image of PHS and a lion in the end zone of the opponent, and found strength to play even harder.

After graduation, I coached at Panhandle High School in Texas, and to put it mildly, PHS did not have a tradition of winning. The other coaches and I wondered how in the world we were going to win a few games this upcoming season and how to build a winning tradition in PHS. After what we considered to be many fruitless suggestions and maybe even considering that it had been a mistake to take a job at PHS, I suggested a victory flag to hang on the flagpole for a week in front of the high school after each win. The head coach said, "Let's go with it."

We ordered a flag from a company in Amarillo that made custom flags. One of the coaches that also taught shop made an oak box with glass in the front to display the flag. We displayed the flag at the swimming pool for about two weeks and then at some stores in town. The talk of the town was our victory flag.

During two-a-days, with the flag displayed in the dressing room, we talked to the players about starting a winning tradition at PHS and flying the victory flag in front of the high school. (Years later, the head coach told me he was afraid the flag might rot before we won a game.)

During our two scrimmages the cheerleaders displayed the flag in front of our fans. By this time, we had created a lot of interest in the victory flag. On the bus trip to the first game, we put the victory flag in one of the front seats of the bus so the players could see it when they got on and off the bus. During the game, it was on a table in front of our fans. Luckily, we won the first game. The other team fumbled, and we recovered the ball on the 10-yard line with seconds left in the game.

As we drove into town after the game, we saw a large group of people gathered around the flagpole in front of the high school. By the time the bus got to the field house behind the high school, the cheerleaders greeted the team as they got off the bus and ushered them to the front of the high school.

Amid much cheering and a speech by the head coach and some of the players, the band played the school song and the victory flag was raised to the top of flagpole. The players, students and fans bought into the idea of the victory flag and, luckily, we had six more after-the-game, flag-raising ceremonies that year.

Over the years, the flag became so important that it was flown for all varsity athletic victories as well as for band, choir, and so forth. The Lions Club won a contest and flew our victory flag at city hall. These examples illustrate how a small idea can—with lots of planning, luck, and sweat—bring a community together and contribute to developing a winning tradition in a school and community. Consider how you may use a victory flag to motivate your team or town.

Four Difficult Motivational Situations

How Do You Motivate When You Have to Deal With Difficult Situations?

Beyond the normal day-to-day issues, each coach encounters all kinds of difficult situations in which he or she has to try to motivate their players. This section provides suggestions for addressing a few of the most common difficult situations. For assistance and guidance in dealing with other issues as they arise, you can contact the authors at Team Up, Inc. (www.teamupsuccess.com)

#1: Overconfidence Sets In

Your team is on a roll, but all of a sudden you notice players are not listening quite as well. They begin to look past what they perceive to be "lesser" opponents.

Answer: The key is to bring them back to reality.

- Remind them of a time they lost to an opponent they should have beaten.

- Show videos of them being less than their best. Also, show them how they can execute to their potential.

- Another option is to set new goals. Push the team to excel even more. Tiger Woods in 1997 wanted to win the Masters golf tournament. After the first three rounds, he was ahead of the field by a very wide margin. To not become complacent, he set his sights on another goal: the largest winning margin ever, which was previously held by Arnold Palmer. Tiger would not be denied and went on to win by 12 shots. Your team may be so good they need to rethink what is possible.

- The best thing is to remind them that playing like a champion means not ever taking any opponent lightly, but always respecting everyone. The opposing team will use your arrogance against you every time and play the underdog role.

- If they are a great team, remember what Elvis said: "T.C.B.—Take Care of Business." Execute like you can. Celebrate later.

- Do not be afraid to pat your team on the back. It is okay to tell them how proud you are of them and how their hard work is paying off

#2: Adversity Hits the Team

What do you do when, from out of nowhere, a tragedy happens? It could be a terrible car accident or debilitating injury during play involving a player or someone close to the team.

Answer: Communicate. Bring the team together and tell them what is going on.

- Show you are concerned about the player and that you will handle the situation as a "family."

- Assure the team that all is being done that can be done by professionals to help deal with the situation.

- Tell them the team must continue and play on. Of course, the person would want the team to play on. This difficult situation does not change team goals, and now, more than ever, you need to lean on each other to be successful and get through this time.

- Be careful. Using the situation as a time to dedicate the season to that person could backfire. Wait and see what happens.
- The key is to communicate, to show concern, and to stay as focused as possible.

#3: A Player Wants to Quit

You could tell the player's enthusiasm was starting to wane, but you didn't realize he was contemplating quitting. Refer back to the section on "Motivating Mr. and Ms. Indifferent" in Chapter 1 for more options.

Answer: Of course, you have several options when a player wants out. You can do what they did in the old days and simply let them go ("You quit, too bad."). However, keep in mind you are sending a message to everyone else on the team. Instead of just letting them go, consider the following:

- Talk to the player and ask him about what is going on. By simply taking the time to talk to the player, you will send the message that he is important to you and does matter. More important, it shows you care. That may turn them around and bring them back into the fold with more enthusiasm than ever.
- You may also find he has serious family issues (or worse) and feels he has no option but quitting. Remember, Coaches coach. Help your player find options to work things out.
- Try to find out why he is quitting. Remember the four main reasons players quit are: (1) not having any fun, (2) feeling the coach only plays their favorites, (3) finding something else they would enjoy more, (4) a misunderstanding and they could have heard something that is totally false. Let them explain.
- Make sure the player had an opportunity to compete. Did he get to feel what it is like to have his adrenaline pumping so fast that he could barely breathe? Did he play in a game, or will he never get that opportunity?
- Remember, the player who quits today can never help contribute tomorrow. Plus, by quitting, it sends the wrong message as a solution to their problems for the rest of their lives. If they quit and are off the team, you cannot have any effect on them.
- Be sure to find the player's "Letter to Myself" and send it to him before your visit. Or, hand it to him because included in that letter are the player's own words and his signature on a commitment that he wont quit—even when things get difficult.

> Bear Bryant said, "Quitting is hard the first time. After that, it gets easier and easier." Giving up on your commitment to your teammates should never be easy.

#4: Your Team Keeps Losing

You have tried everything, and nothing seems to work. The losses are piling up and enthusiasm is way down.

Answer: Keep in mind everyone is watching to see if you give up and throw in the towel.

- Stay positive. Others will be quick to criticize and gripe. Let them do that, but set an example that you are going to be positive and that you have a plan to get things back on course. Then, go back to the basics of coaching. One player, one play at a time. Execute and remember: you are a team.

- The success of your season is not solely determined by your win-loss record. Keep in mind: you are building for the future.

- Celebrate any kind of small victory. Set realistic goals that players can reach, and then go after bigger ones.

- Use the object lesson of the "snowball fight" to constructively get out your collective frustrations.

- Go back to the basics. What does a baseball pitcher do when he's lost it? Not only can he no longer fire the ball over the plate a hundred miles an hour, he can't even find the plate and is just launching watermelons. The pitcher, in thought, should go back to his old neighborhood to his old backyard and pick up a tattered baseball. At first, he will simply toss it into the air getting his feel back, like a child playing. Then slowly he will pick out a spot on the side of the garage and begin to throw a little bit until he gets his "feel" back. Next, he will see an old tire swinging and will begin throwing the ball again and again getting better and more accurate with each throw. Suddenly he is firing the ball like he once did and his confidence soars. Now, without even thinking about it, he's ready to go back and face the batter. Sometimes, we all need to go back to the basics and start over.

3

How to Set Goals and
Stay on Track

Setting Team Goals

> "Knowing where you are going is the first step to getting there."
> —Ken Blanchard

Ken Blanchard (author of numerous books, including *The One Minute Manager*) perfectly describes the problem confronting many players and coaches today—wanting to win but often not knowing how to get there.

The reality is: every team and every player must have goals to hit if they want to achieve anything of value, which includes both short-term and long-term goals. While everyone wants to get to state or win a championship, the truth is: the only way to hit long-term goals is to achieve the short-term goals first. In his book, *Power Exchange*, Lee Colan reminds readers: "When you help players see how they fit into the big picture, they naturally feel more accountable for their performance when they are clearly part of something bigger than themselves."

Smart coaches explain their goals by consistently answering the four questions all players and assistant coaches ask:

- What are we trying to achieve?
- How are we going to achieve it?
- How can I contribute?
- What's in it for me?

Everyone wants to know what the goals are and how they will achieve those goals, especially the new generation of players today. Today's athletes, however, also have an additional question: they want to know why. Coaches can no longer just tell players what to do. Their players also want to know why and how—once players understand these aspects of the goals, they will likely get on board and give their all.

What the players and coaches really want you to explain are:

- The goals: clearly defined
- The plans: detailed, clear steps required to achieve the goals

> "Great leaders never tell people what to do. They set clear goals and establish parameters. Lousy leaders think they know it all and all the while their organization sits there, missing their potential."
> —General Norman Schwarzkopf

- The roles: broad—yet clear—performance expectations
- The rewards: benefits for the player or coach

With the commitment coaches expect of their players, a specific plan and expectations are well worth the effort. In addition to setting goals for the preseason and the full season, you should also set weekly goals. You will also need to determine how you will communicate the goals to the team. When setting goals, keep in mind the following:

- For your team to reach its potential, you need to be clear in your team goals before you move on to the individual goals.

- Obviously things change during a season. However, what should not change are your set goals and the plan to be successful.

- In deciding your goals, be sure to consult with others who can contribute their expertise and insight. In the end, they will be the ones implementing the plan to hit the goals, anyway.

Coaches often make the mistake of thinking everyone is on board and knows where the team is headed. A Harris Poll of 11,000 families found the following:

- Only 15 percent of workers could identify their organization's most important goals.

- A majority of workers (51 percent) did not understand what they were supposed to do to help the organization achieve its goals.

- Less than half of valuable work time (49 percent) was spent on the organization's most important goals.

> "Set high goals and be positive so others who share your goals will work together to attain them."
>
> —Jody Conradt, former head coach, University of Texas—the winningest coach in women's collegiate basketball history

Do Your Players Know What Your Team Goals Are?

To make sure your bases are covered:

- Have your players write out your team goals. Plain and simple, make sure they know what your intentions are for the season, for the week, and for them personally. This book includes goal sheets for the coach, the team, and individual players.

- Think about it: both the sun and a laser give off light. A laser uses a weaker source of energy and focuses it in a cohesive stream of light to produce intense heat and power. With a laser, you can drill a hole in a diamond—that is the power of focus.

- Ask your players to write down and focus on your season's goals, your weekly goals, and their personal goals. Leave no room for confusion.

Once you have thought through your team goals and developed a plan for communicating them, you are now ready to help individual players realize what they need to do to achieve those goals. Coach Frank Kush said, "You have to set realistic goals for each player. You must set short-term goals (two to three weeks), intermediate goals (a month or two), and long-term goals (full season)." Coach Kush continued by saying, "One of the biggest problems I ran into as a young coach was when I first started, I thought every player was going to be a superstar. I found out they weren't and I had to set realistic goals for each player."

Make Sure Your Players Set Realistic Goals That Are Significant.

Another good reason to have players write down short-term goals is that when they achieve some of their small or easier milestones, it motivates them and they will be ready to go after more. Coach Ron Shipper says, "We want the player to look at himself honestly and say, 'What can I do to become a better player? What can I do to become a better team member?' Each person must sit down and ask those questions of himself."

This self-reflection is not always a simple task. All of us want to be the superstars seen on TV, but the reality is everyone can't be a superstar. Each person can, however, contribute to the team goals. Being a role player is not a bad position to be in because you contribute to the team's success. After all, each player is one turned ankle from being a starter. Coach Hughes from Dunbar High School in Fort Worth, Texas, said he prepares 12 players to play in each game. When a player who would usually not get in the game for other teams was interviewed, he said, "I know I will get in the game if for only a few minutes, and I have to be ready to get a steal or an important rebound to help my team." Everyone needs realistic goals and can help the team.

The number-one reason kids drop out of sports is they lose interest. They simply do not have clear goals or any direction. Do you know of anyone who has "flunked out" of Yale or Harvard? The answer is probably no, but the actual reason is that these schools don't give Fs. At Yale and Harvard, the faculty believes it is their responsibility to help the student graduate. If the student is smart enough to get accepted, the reality is they can't fail. They may just take a while longer to complete their course work.

What if coaches took the same responsibility in helping student-athletes reach their individual goals? Kids would love to have someone so interested in them. They could help each player determine what their potential really is and begin realizing it long before they graduated from high school.

> "I would meet with players individually to talk about the goals they had set for themselves. If the player's goals were unrealistic, I would tone them down and explain what it would take to reach the goals the player had written down. Every player kept a copy of his goals and if there was ever an occasion concerning a discipline matter, I pulled out the player's stated goals and told him if his current behavior continued, it would be impossible for him to reach his stated goals."
>
> —Grant Teaff, Baylor University

Team Goals: "Who is Our Gipper?"

Many are familiar with the story of the 1929 Notre Dame "Fighting Irish" football team and how they dedicated their season to George Gipp. George was a varsity athlete at the University of Notre Dame from 1917 to 1920. While planning to pursue a career in baseball, he was convinced by legendary college coach Knute Rockne to play football. He led the Fighting Irish to a 27-2-3 record, playing both offense and defense. Several of his records still stand today.

But how did the saying "Win one for the Gipper!" come about? Well, here's the sad part of the story. It seems that George developed a severe throat infection during one of his final football games at Notre Dame. He died a few weeks later at the age of 25. Just before he died, he told Coach Rockne: "Some time, Rock, when the team is up against it, when things are wrong and the breaks are beating the boys, tell them to go in there with all they've got and win just one for the Gipper. I don't know where I'll be then, Rock, but I'll know about it and I'll be happy."

What will motivate us? Often, as the season progresses (or even in pre-season), the question becomes, "Who or what does this team play for?" Of course, Notre Dame had George Gipp, but stop and think about what motivates your team to give their all. One team in Arkansas answers this question by having each player bring down one person onto the field before the game. The player tells the person when they step onto the field, "Tonight, _____, I am playing for you." The other person then wishes them well and goes back to their seat. Can you imagine how both parties must feel and what a difference this approach could make in the players' effort?

Coach Tom Beauchamp of Lindbergh High School in St. Louis uses a variation of this technique by having his players present their away jersey to someone special for them to wear at home games. Many players pick a teacher or family member, and Coach Beauchamp says, "It's a big deal when you ask someone to wear your jersey and you know you are playing for more than yourself."

Goals really are the key to this motivation. However, be careful not to make your goals too large or too unrealistic. The problem with huge, season-long goals—like to win a state championship—is they often become de-motivated if the team loses even a single game. Then, the season becomes futile because the players already realize they have missed their goal. One veteran college coach decided to motivate his team by tacking up a banner that read, "Our one goal: to win our conference." However, after two defeats in conference play, the team began giving up, not only on game day, but all through the week during practices.

T.E.A.M. Goals

Better motivating goals are T.E.A.M. goals for the season. These are goals that are discussed, that you execute with a specific plan, that others "buy into," and with which you can stay motivated.

- **T:** Talk and Discuss
- **E:** Execute
- **A:** Acceptance
- **M:** Motivate

T: Talk and Discuss

It is important for everyone to discuss what the realistic goals are for the season. Head coaches must discuss with assistant coaches and others about what expectations they have. Of course, not every year is going to be a championship season, even though your players can play like champions and model championship behaviors—on and off the field.

What do you talk about and discuss? Evaluations of the players, the schedule, and the intangibles—such as the level of the team's experience—are the topics of discussion. Is the majority of the team made up of freshman? Is this the coach's first few years with a new system? Is it a team made up of seniors who barely missed out on going all the way the season before? The key is to communicate and think through what you have to work with. Then you are ready to develop a plan.

Execute

What is your plan to reach the goals? Who is responsible for helping you reach your expectations? Don't think about just the assistant coaches. Are there others you can receive input from? Part of your plan should be weekly goals just like the players have on their goal sheets. (See the next section.) On your team goal sheet, you should have goals that you want to accomplish in spring drills, pre-season, each week, and the season. Your weekly goals should elevate play, be a reminder of what needs to be worked on, and your plan to beat your next opponent.

> "If you sacrifice early, you'll win late."
>
> —Charles Haley

Acceptance

Now that you have discussed your goals with others and have come up with your plan, your next step is to get acceptance. Your goals and plan will be meaningless if you don't get the team's "buy in" or acceptance. A suggested three-step process to get everyone on board would be:

- *Evaluation:* Assistant coaches need to help head coaches give an honest evaluation of the players. To motivate a player, the individual goal must be obtainable. Once this coaches' meeting for evaluations has taken place, you are ready to meet with the players.

- *Private Meetings*: Have a private meeting with every player before the season begins. At that time, you and the player will come up with their specific expectations and goals. The player will not work hard enough to achieve anything special if he is not part of the process. Ask the player what he thinks about your season and what they can contribute. Remember, Generation Y really likes to be consulted when decisions are being made. Using the player's goal sheet, which has been provided, determine the player's specific goals and *the player's specific plan to make this happen*. Have him fill out his sheet in a private session.

- *Commitment Announcements:* Take the information and commitments made from the coaches and players and begin to fill out your team goal sheet. Filling out the team goal sheet without meeting with everyone first would be "putting the cart before the horse." An excellent idea would be to follow-up the private player's meetings with a team-building event or outing to seal and announce everyone's commitment.

For example, as Grant Teaff developed the Secret Society of the Gold Dot, you could use something like "Crossing the Rubicon" as a way for everyone to make a commitment to what you want to accomplish. The best event is something unique that also fits your team. You can also adopt one of the team mottos provided here or come up with your own as a battle cry.

Motivate

Now that your team has set and accepted your goals and plan of action, you are ready to motivate. The only way your team will reach its goals is if the following conditions are met:

- You, as the coach, stay motivated.
- You motivate the other assistant coaches.
- You and the assistant coaches motivate the players.
- The players motivate each other.

This book is filled with all the tools you need. Plus, you have great experiences of your own in your arsenal. You have been part of winning teams as well as teams that didn't perform as well.

Remember, the outcome of every season isn't always about the talent. Ask Guy Lewis, who coached the University of Houston in the 1983 NCAA basketball game against N.C. State. Houston had much better talent than their opponent and yet they came up short.

You get those average players to play great by motivating them and helping them see things in themselves they don't see or have never seen. Be creative in your motivation. You can find all kinds of ways to get the best out of your teams. On a day when you don't think they are trying their hardest or they're not working together, try something out of the ordinary.

> "The key to winning is getting the average players to play good and the good players to play great!"
>
> —Bum Phillips

If you are a football coach, get one of the biggest blocking sleds you can find. Tell the players to gather around and then tell one of the smaller players to come up and move the blocking sled with you on it. He, of course, will look at you like you're crazy, but encourage him to give it a try. After he struggles a few moments, you then say, "Okay. Now I want you _____ (pick the guy laughing the most) to give it a try and bring _____ with you." The two will do better, but they still will not be able to move it like you want. Then you say, "That's how we looked in practice today. It was lackluster. Some good effort, but we didn't work together and share the load."

Now you bring up two more players to help, and, of course, the sled should move easily. Next, tell them, "Okay, now that's what I am talking about. That's how we will hit our goals—by working together. When we work as a team, we don't sing solos, we sound like a whole orchestra! See you tomorrow!"

The T.E.A.M. goals form (Figure 3-1) will help you focus on the direction of your team. Each coach should fill out the form and have a realistic plan of action. This form will help you set a course and stay on track.

Randy Pench / Zuma Press

T.E.A.M. Goals Form

(to be filled out by the coach)

1. Who have you discussed the pre-season goals with? _____
_____

2. What off-season goals do you have? _____
_____

3. What extra effort will it take to reach your goals? _____
_____

4. From what you learned in preseason, how do you see your team shaping up and what goals do you have now? _____
_____

5. Who do you need to talk with to help determine what the team's potential is? _____
_____

6. What plan have you come up with to help you reach your goals? List four things that you consider a major part of your plan:

   1. _____

   2. _____

   3. _____

   4. _____

7. Have you met with the players to look at their goals? _____

8. Do you have "buy in" from everyone on your plan? _____

   Who do you need to get more commitment from to be successful? _____
_____

9. How are you going to motivate your team to reach the goals everyone has committed to? List five special things you are committing to do that will help:

   1. _____

   2. _____

   3. _____

   4. _____

   5. _____

10. What are the de-motivators your team has to be aware of and avoid? _____
_____

Figure 3-1. T.E.A.M. Goals Form

Player's Goal Evaluation Form

Player will set goals and be evaluated in size, speed, muscle development, vertical jump, attitude, ability to learn, agility, desire, leadership, guts, and teamwork.

Player's Name _____ Age _____

Grade _____

Date filled out _____ Next evaluation date _____

Player's stated goals for season (be specific): _____

_____

Player and coach's plan of action to reach goals: _____

_____

Size: Player's current weight _____

What size would the player like to achieve to be more successful? _____

Speed: In the 40-yard dash, how fast is the athlete now? _____

- Excellent speed: 4.8
- Good: 4.9 to 5.2
- Average: 5.3 to 5.6
- Slow: 5.7 or more

What is the athlete's goal? _____

How will he reach this goal? _____

Strength: Current weight player can bench press? _____ Goal _____

Current weight player can squat? _____ Goal _____

Current weight player can power lift? _____ Goal _____

Vertical Jump for Explosion: Current height _____ Goal _____

	Ability to Learn	Desire	Attitude	Leadership	Guts	Teamwork
Poor	0	0	0	0	0	0
Fair	1	1	1	1	1	1
Good	2	2	2	2	2	2
Excellent	3	3	3	3	3	3

Grades: Student's GPA _____ Student's Goal GPA _____

What will keep the student on track? _____

Player's signature _____ Date _____

Coach's signature _____ Date_____

Figure 3-2. Player's Goal Evaluation Form

Player's Goal Sheet: Its Purpose and Use

At the beginning of the season, ask each athlete to write down his goals. Also ask them to evaluate themselves to see if they are on pace to reach their goals. On the player's goal evaluation form (Figure 3-2) is a place for a coach to evaluate the player. The player will fill out the form before the season starts. The coach then calls in the players, one-on-one, and evaluates them, going over each area and explaining why the player is being graded high or low.

Keep in mind: This form is meant to be a motivational tool. Players will generally be harder on themselves when they grade themselves. Coaches need to be realistic when they help the student-athlete objectively look at themselves and their abilities.

- With the coach's help, the players should acknowledge what areas they need to work on if they are to hit their goals. Always finish the evaluation by saying something complimentary or positive about the athlete.

- Be as specific and positive as possible, and leave each athlete with the idea that if he or she works on the specific areas you have encouraged them to work on, they will be much better athletes and individuals able to contribute to the team's goals even more.

- Ask your student-athletes *how* they plan to hit the goals you have discussed. In other words, have each one share their plan of action with you while making a verbal commitment.

- Players should be individually evaluated three times during the year for the greatest impact of this exercise.

- This evaluation form, which can be found on the following page, was originally developed and graciously shared by Wichita Falls High School and their former head coach, Leo Brittain. Changes can be made to include additional areas you may want your athletes to spend time on for their personal development.

4

How to Build a True Team

Jed Jacobsohn / Getty Images Sport

The V.I.C.T.O.R.Y. System

How can you turn a group of individuals into a true team? Every coach wrestles with how he can take a group of players and mold them into a cohesive unit. Following is a method to help you create what Bill Curry calls "the miracle of team." Follow this step-by-step process and begin to enjoy what it feels like when you know you truly are there for each other and can accomplish anything. The CEO at the Outback Steakhouse Golf Tournament recently said, "Teamwork—it's the difference between a we/us experience and an I/me experience. We/us is a better way."

This simple seven-step process is called V.I.C.T.O.R.Y. because that's what every team is after:

- V: Vision
- I: Inclusion
- C: Competition
- T: Teamwork
- O: Obtainable Goals
- R: Respect
- Y: "Yes We Can" Attitude

Vision

It all begins with vision. Visionaries are able to see things that others don't—both in individuals and groups of people. Visionaries see not only potential, but more importantly they also see end results even before the first whistle has been blown. The vision will differ depending on the situation. It may be for a winning season for the first time in 10 years or for an elusive state championship. While the coach or leader may be the first to see the vision, soon others will gravitate to the excitement and opportunity. Good visionaries can paint the picture and prepare the group for the next step.

What is the vision for your team? Are your expectations realistic? Make sure to ask others what they "see" for your team. Find an effective way to relay the message. Be aware of any potential roadblocks as you present your vision.

Inclusion

Inclusion means being sure you have included everyone possible to begin achieving the vision. Black, white, Hispanic, Asian, seniors, sophomores, rich, and poor—it doesn't matter. Everyone should feel included and have the opportunity to compete. Players will come together and start to feel a kinship. They will grasp the clear vision, buy into the realistic goal and begin getting excited. Basic needs of being included are met, overriding any differences. People wonder why so many intercity kids gravitated to gangs. The reality is that they feel included like nowhere else. Isolation is the worst kind of punishment. To include someone can become magical. Vince Lombardi reminds us, "Regardless of personal accomplishments, the only true satisfaction a player receives is the satisfaction that only comes from being part of a successful team." The good news is, sports meets this need, and once they see the vision and feel appreciated, they are ready for the next step—to compete with their new team.

Include all players who are eligible to participate. One high school coach said, "I know there are a lot of great wide receivers just walking the halls." Today with the numbers dropping in participation, coaches must recruit in their own schools. It is obviously in a coach's best interest to ensure that everyone available feels they have an opportunity to be on the team and compete for a position.

Keep in mind, Michael Jordan was cut in the ninth grade from his high school basketball team. Do you think he may have been overlooked? Make sure you and your staff help your players realize they are valued members of the team, even though they may not play as much as the starters?

The best way to help all players feel included is to give them recognition when you see good performances and solid effort. When you acknowledge good play, you will reinforce the good behavior and players will continue to give their best.

Remember the players you walk past today may be the starters you rely on tomorrow.

                                                              —Unknown

---

Competition

Once players see the vision and feel like a part of the team, they are ready to compete. The old adage is true: nothing brings a team together quite like a common foe. Coaches love game day. In developing this book, we interviewed many retired coaches who could not stop talking about what it was like to get ready on game day and the excitement of the game itself. Players feel the same way. They can't sleep the night before because they are so excited. Competing is fun, and players—all players—need the opportunity to get a taste. Too often, coaches (and everyone else) place so much emphasis on winning that the real reasons kids play get lost. Athletes want to compete. They want to feel the rush of adrenaline and improve their performance.

Set up your practices so as to keep the competitive juices flowing. Arrange scrimmages with other teams, and take players to see other teams in action. How can you be sure all of your players get into competition? Give players a taste of the competition they crave and they will excel. You can provide players with the rush of competition in many different ways, as the following example illustrates. In 2006, because of past infractions, Baylor University and their new men's basketball coach Scott Drew were not allowed to play any out-of-conference games. Coach Drew set up scrimmages with alumni players who came in from around the country and even took his team to Dallas to play at the American Airlines Center so they would remember what it is like to compete.

> "Accept the challenge so that you may feel the exhilaration of victory."
> —George Patton

Teamwork

Teamwork has been described many ways. Ultimately, it is about sacrifice. Teamwork has nothing to do with the individual, and then again, it has everything to do with the individual. Teamwork has nothing to do with the individual because you sacrifice individual statistics and self-accolades for the team. The team functions as a military unit with a clear goal in mind and together can achieve the extraordinary. Individually, people can't always achieve their expectations, yet as a team, a group of individuals bound together, they can make obstacles fall.

By itself, twine is not very strong. However, when braided together to form rope, one piece can hold 100 times its weight. In the end, teamwork has everything to do with the individual because the individual brings his unique gifts and talents to the table. Then, when meshed with the gifts and talents of the other team members, confidence soars.

What happens in building a team is character begins to develop from lessons learned while working unselfishly with others, which lasts a lifetime. Ultimately, the individual realizes the individual self is no match to the abilities of the team and begins to work with others. All the while, the player finds out that teamwork is not only more productive, it is also more fun.

> "I've had records in the past, and that's not what satisfies me. What drives me is team success and getting better as an individual to make the team better, doing whatever it takes to win games."
>
> —Jackie Stiles, number-one scorer in women's college basketball history (*Sports Leaders & Success*)

> "It's the miracle of teamwork. It is a miracle because you have black and white, rich and poor battling side by side. You find out your blood is the same color as theirs and your sweat smells exactly the same. America comes together in sports and barriers come down."
>
> —Coach Bill Curry

To turn your group into a true team, make sure your team is working together for common goals. When you go through the steps outlined in the previous sections, you should have little doubt that you are starting to become a team. When you offer clear vision, include everyone, and allow players to compete, then they are starting to become a team. If your group is still lacking in one of these areas, they have not reached their full potential. Webster's defines teamwork as: "work done by a number of associates usually with each doing a clearly defined portion but all subordinating personal prominence to the efficiency of the whole." Clearly stated: players sacrifice to help the team win.

Obtainable Goals

Zig Ziglar, America's preeminent motivational speaker, said during a speech at the AFCA meeting in Dallas in 2006, "While I believe in the power of positive thinking, I don't believe in unrealistic expectations." He went on to point out that Shaquille O'Neal is a great basketball player; however, with all the positive thinking in the world, he would never make a good horse jockey. While the crowd howled, the truth is clear: people must all be realistic in their expectations. Parents, of course, are notorious for having unrealistic expectations of their children. Indeed, you must have goals, otherwise you will spend all your time fighting fires and solving problems. Of course, you need season goals as well as weekly goals. The key is having a bull's-eye to shoot for. Have individual, realistic goals that are written down and that players feel are obtainable.

Goals are like a map for a team and a player. The player must see the target in order to hit it and be truly successful. Coach Ron Schipper was asked how he could develop winning attitudes with players that are positive and that will develop and mean something to them. "I believe it starts with setting goals. You want the player to look at himself honestly and say, 'What can I do to become a better football player? What can I do to become a better team member?' Each person must sit down and ask those questions of himself." Coach Schipper fully understands the importance of setting realistic obtainable goals that motivate players.

> "If you have goals that are reachable, they will reach and succeed."
>
> —Unknown

Respect

One of the most important things any coach can do in building a true team is to teach respect. Respect really means, "having high or special regard." In other words, honor those deserving. Coaches certainly deserve respect. No coach is in the profession because of money. Team Up has found coach after coach who gives so much of himself because he loves the game and wants to help children. Certainly that type of dedication is deserving of respect.

Players deserve respect because they give of themselves. Players practice in 100-degree heat, work odd jobs because their families need the money, practice their sport, and even manage study time—just to compete. Respect can be shown in many forms:

- Tell people you appreciate them.
- Act like you respect them, being respectful of their feelings and time.
- Show them you respect them by asking about their families and lives.
- Praise in public; chastise in private.

One of life's most important lessons can be summed up by remembering the following: if you want respect, give respect. Again, people remember what you do more than what you say. To become a true team, respect must be a cornerstone of the team—players respecting coaches, coaches respecting players, and players respecting players. Each component must exist for the team to excel. To which of your players do you specifically need to show your respect? Coaches and players need to learn that to get respect you must give it. True teammates respect each other and appreciate each other's commitment. Never allow players to talk about or degrade one another. It simply tears at the fabric of the team. Keep in mind it is hard enough to compete with your opponents, let alone your teammates. Fighting in the barracks does nothing but weaken the army.

"Yes, We Can" Attitude

Every team must have an attitude that is positive. Of course, it starts with the leader. Do you have a positive, can-do attitude? Players look for positive role models, and coaches may be the best examples your players encounter. With the number of parents not available, players look to coaches to set the tone. Keep in mind, Generation Y is generally very optimistic and expect the same from its leaders. Also, keep in mind that the title of this section is "Yes. We Can" Attitude. It takes the whole team, everyone encouraging each other, to get the job done.

Three men were busting rocks one day on a construction site. Someone asked the first fellow, "What are you doing?" He replied, "I am busting rocks." They asked the second guy, "What are you doing?" And he replied, "Busting rocks, it's my job. I do it from 7:00 in the morning until I quit at 6:00." Then they asked the last person busting rocks, "What are you doing?" And he replied, "I am building a cathedral." Attitude is everything. It totally depends on how you look at things.

Showing You Care: Building a True Team Starts With Caring

"No player ever has enough skill to overcome a bad attitude."
—Mildred "Lanky" Lancaster

A coach's greatest tool is understanding that every player wants to please someone. They want to please a person whom they know cares. Showing them you care can and will make a difference. To build a true team, the leaders must show players they really care about them. If the players feel true concern, they will listen and follow the leader anywhere. Following are some tips on how to show the players you really care:

- Ask your players about themselves and their families.
- Smile at them and even laugh together.
- Ask them what they think.
- Show them you trust them by allowing them to make decisions.
- Talk to them about being "champions" in life—not just in sports.
- When you see players doing something well, tell them.
- Take time to coach them and show them a better way of doing something.
- Hold them accountable for what they do. Teach them their choices have consequences.
- Treat them fairly and equally—even the star players.
- Listen to them, and have an open-door policy.

When asked how he wanted to be remembered during the Gulf War, General Norman Schwarzkopf said that he loved his family, he loved his troops, and they loved him. Schwarzkopf knew that if he truly cared about his troops, they would follow him anywhere—even into war. Who do you need to make sure knows you care for them?

"People don't care how much you know until they know how much you care."
—Lou Holtz

Team Mottos

The best team mottos are those that develop naturally during the course of competition and the team coming together. When coming up with a motto, think of what your team stands for and its goals. However, following are some examples of mottos from a number of teams:

- Protect the Tradition (Southlake Carroll High School, Southlake, Texas)
- The Beast of the East (Clovis High School, Clovis, New Mexico)
- There Ain't Nothing Tougher Than a Wildcat (Clovis High School, Clovis, New Mexico)
- Through These Doors Walk the Hardest Working Players in Texas (Permian High School, Odessa, Texas)
- Anyone, Anywhere, Anytime (Army Rangers)
- Tradition Never Graduates (Artesia High School, Artesia, New Mexico)
- Never Without Honor (USMC)
- Play Like a Champion Today (University of Notre Dame)
- Second Sucks (Livingston)
- Refuse 2 Lose
- Whatever It Takes
- Aim High
- Free Trip to State—Details Inside (on a sign over the weight room)
- Perfect Practice Makes Perfect (Lou Holtz)
- FLC: Fight Like Champions
- 48 Minutes to Play, A Lifetime of Memories
- To Be the Best, You Gotta Beat the Best
- Hard Work Beats Talent When Talent Won't Work Hard (University of Oklahoma)
- "Being part of this program has serious side effects. They include numerous victories, loud celebrations, Heisman Trophy winners, high draft picks, and a permanent addiction to being a 'Cane." (Miami Hurricanes)
- Outhit, Outhustle, Outscore!
- The Time Is Now
- OTSS: Only the Strong Survive
- Summon the Magic

- Together We Stand, Together We Fall, Together We Win, and Winners Take All!
- Good Is the Enemy of Great (from the book Good To Great by Jim Collins)
- Desire—I *Want* to Be the Best I Can! Dedication—I *Will* Work Hard to Be the Best I Can! Determination—I *Will* Be the Best I Can!
- Goals Without Commitment Are Nothing More Than Dreams.
- Rise Up!
- 98.7: The Exact Mileage to a State Championship
- You Really Don't Know What You Can Do
- Let's Step It Up!
- Let's Reach Out and Let's Become More Than We Were Yesterday.
- You Are Either Going Forward or Backward. Seldom Are You Going to Stay the Same.
- How Do You Move Forward? By Working Hard.
- Speed, Spirit, Skill, and Poise (Gordon Wood)
- If It's To Be, It's Up to Me (Vince Dooley of University of Georgia)
- All Out, All the Time (Dunbar High School, Fort Worth, Texas)
- The Secret Is: Effort, Plain and Simple

Photo From University of Notre Dame

A Motivational Vocabulary

Every team has its own identity. Motivational words will help define your team. Use them in all kinds of motivational ways—especially as an acronym when spelling out your school name or mascot. For example, if your school mascot is the pirate, you can use the words this way:

- P: Practice
- I: Intense
- R: Respect
- A: Achieve
- T: Teamwork
- E: Enthusiasm
- S: Success

Be creative with the alphabetical motivational vocabulary:

- A: Achieve, awards, attitude, accolades, accomplishments, atmosphere, action
- B: Build, basics, believe, becoming, belonging, benefit
- C: Champion, community, commitment, cohesion, character, create, competition, communicate, choices, consistent, confidence, challenge, conquer
- D: Dedicate, determination, develop, demanding, drill, decide, dare, defeat, defense, demand, demonstrate, depth, desire, destiny, dream, drive, dynasty, dependable
- E: Effort, encouragement, exceptional, exemplary, example, enthusiasm, eager, earn, execute, edge, effort, eliminate, empower, example, expect, explosive
- F: Focus, fight, finish, foundation, faith, fun, fundamentals, fate, fast, fierce, fiery
- G: Goal, growth, game, gain, gladiator, glory, gratitude, grid iron, guts
- H: Heart, hero, humor, hustle, hard noised, harness, history, honest, hope, humble
- I: Inspiring, ignite, intangible, imagine, immovable, imposing, indispensable, intense
- J: Journey, job, joy, jubilant, justice, justify, join
- K: Knowledge, kindle, knock, knife, kick, kind, knight
- L: Loyalty, leadership, love, labor, landmark, last, launch, legend, lethal
- M: Motivation, mandate, manage, manpower, marathon, master, meaning, more

- N: Noble, now, new, necessity, neighbor, non stop, nothing less, never, name, need
- O: Opportunity, objective, option, ongoing, outlook, operation, obey, one, optimist
- P: Prepare, practice, plan, prevent, promote, positive, pride, potential, principles, produce, prevail
- Q: Quality, quench, quest
- R: Respect, recognize, remember, responsible, reality, race, rave, reorganize, reach, reliability
- S: Spirit, sacrifice, strong, skills, sharing, strength, success, satisfy, succeed, seize
- T: Teamwork, team, together, teach, talent, tempest, terrific, think, TNT, tough, triumph
- U: Unify, unselfish, understanding, urgency, unbeaten, underdog, unstoppable
- V: Victory, values, validate, valuable, valiant, versatile, victorious, vision
- W: Work, we, willing, win, weapon, willing, wisdom
- X: X-ray, x-traordinary (we know it is a reach)
- Y: Yearn, youth, yes, your
- Z: Zest, zeal, zone

Team-Building Topics

Legendary Coach Gordon Wood created what he called "The High Listening Period" as a way to involve his players in motivating the rest of the team. During this time, the team came together and one player would speak on one of many topics. The five-minute session (they strictly adhered to the five-minute timeframe) was not always a speech. Often, it was an interactive time, ranging from playing Simon Says to telling jokes. Generally, these times were serious and occurred every day before the players suited up. During the latter part of the season, seniors spoke, and each player was free to choose their topic. At other times, the coaches would ask the players to address a particular topic. Following are some of the topics discussed:

- Winners (what it means, what it takes to be one, profile of a winner, and who are some winners)
- Losers (what it means, what it takes to be one, profile of a loser, and who are losers)
- Competition (what it means, why compete, what it takes, why it should be exhilarating)

Player's Profile

Name _____

Contact Information: Home Phone _____ Cell Phone _____

Parents' Name(s) _____

Phone Number _____ Cell Phone _____

Grade _____ Birthday _____

Who do you live with? Please list everyone in your house, and include ages of brothers and sisters. _____

Who will be in the stands cheering for you? _____

Position you would like to play? _____

Greatest sports moment before this team experience? _____

_____

What jobs have you held before? _____

_____

Favorite class in school _____

What is your grade-point average (or GPA)? _____

What are your future goals? _____

Have you had other family members go to college? _____

Favorite movie _____

Favorite book _____

Who is your hero? _____ Why?_____

What motivates you to succeed? _____

_____

When you have a difficult decision to make, who would you talk to? _____

_____

What realistic goals do you have for your team? _____

_____

What would a great season look like? _____

_____

What do you need to work on to grow, personally? _____

_____

To be a better player, what must you do?_____

_____

Figure 4-1. Player's profile

Player's Profile

Circle the number which best describes you:

Carefree	1 2 3 4 5 6 7 8 9 10	Serious
Talkative	1 2 3 4 5 6 7 8 9 10	Quiet
Thick-skinned	1 2 3 4 5 6 7 8 9 10	Thin-skinned
Energetic	1 2 3 4 5 6 7 8 9 10	Laid Back
Leader	1 2 3 4 5 6 7 8 9 10	Follower
Mature	1 2 3 4 5 6 7 8 9 10	Growing
Shy	1 2 3 4 5 6 7 8 9 10	Outgoing
Direct	1 2 3 4 5 6 7 8 9 10	Reserved
Steady	1 2 3 4 5 6 7 8 9 10	Flashy
Teammate	1 2 3 4 5 6 7 8 9 10	Individual

If you had one word to describe yourself, what would it be? _____

What is something you don't like? _____

_____

What is an obstacle you have had to overcome in your life? _____

_____

What did you do to overcome your issue?_____

_____

What is something very positive the coaching staff should know about you? _____

_____

Anything else you'd like to add?_____

_____

_____

_____

_____

_____

_____

_____

_____

_____

Figure 4-1. Player's profile (continued)

- Courage (what it is, why is it important, how is it exhibited)
- Intensity (what is it, why is it important, and what are the results)
- Work (define it, why is it important, what does it consist of, what are the results)
- Character (what is it, what it does for you, how is it developed, and why improve it—as well as examples of who you think shows good character)
- Importance of Athletics (what being an athlete means—to you, the school, your community)
- Respect (of yourself, teammates, coaches, elders, school, and community)
- Criticism (what is it, how is it used, how should it be given and taken, results from it)
- Enthusiasm (what is it, who has it, results from it, why it is important, how it should be used)
- Faith (what is it)
- Desire (what is it, importance of it, results from it)
- Imagination (what is it, what are the results from it)
- Decision-Making (what is it, why is it important, what if we don't do it)
- Pride (what is it, what are the results of it)
- Will Power (what is it, what can it help you do)
- Guts (what is it, how is it developed)
- Teamwork (what is it, why is it important)
- Practice (what is it, what comes from it)

Nothing is more motivating than hearing a peer speak about these topics. A variation of this technique is to do exactly what happened in Brownwood. Invite a leader from each school team or club in to hear the topics and then return to report the message to everyone in their own club or team. The key to making this motivational exercise effective is to allow the students time to prepare and encourage them to speak from their hearts.

Player's Profile: Really Getting to Know the Players

This tool is excellent to really get to know your players. Ask them to fill out the player's profile form (Figure 4-1) at the start of the season. Then place it in their folder. Look particularly at the player's personality to know the most effective way to motivate them. Each player will fill out this form, then it will go in your player's file in your coach's office.

5

How to Build Character

Charles Small / Zuma Press

Motivation Through Character Building

"We are on the field and in the locker room to teach our players how to win—not just on the gridiron, but in any profession they choose. We want to impart habits that will lead them to excellence throughout their lives. Most of all, we want to teach them the value of loyalty, integrity, and teamwork. Once you know how to work with people, you can accomplish anything."

—Lou Holtz

As coaches in today's world, we see all kinds of kids in all sorts of situations who need our caring and guidance. As a coach, building character may be the most important job you will ever have. Long after players leave your school and move into the next chapters of their lives, the wisdom and example of strong character you left with each one can make the difference between their success and failure, their happiness or cynicism in life.

Webster's defines character as "a trait or distinctive combination of traits." Truly that's what coaches strive to do, to help kids develop a "combination of traits." A coach's job is not just trying to help kids to be honest or trustworthy or even hardworking, but all the above and at the same time.

Our parents hopefully helped instill these "traits" in us. However, many parents today may not always be available to teach and nurture. So, whose voices will these kids hear when it comes to issues like choosing between right and wrong or competing honorably? The reality is that it often comes back to others—like coaches, youth ministers, and teachers. It seems many high-profile professional athletes either don't want the responsibility or haven't yet gotten their own act together. So, the task of shaping and molding a player's character often comes back to their teachers and coaches, and the responsibility is crucial, not only for the individual's life, but also for our society.

"My coaching philosophy has always been different, and after the accident, it's been accepted as being different. I utilize the physical component to back up what I see initially. I coach the person first, and the event second."

—Bev Kearney, coach of the University of Texas women's track team, who learned to walk again after a crippling traffic accident.

How can you help build character in your players and what are the character traits you need to help them mold? Sports provide a natural arena for teaching or role-modeling character. Of course, in some instances, sports have brought out the worst in people. The good news is that in sports, many opportunities are available for coaches to teach positive traits and help kids do the "right thing." Although many players understand it is a privilege to play sports and it takes discipline, sacrifice, and commitment. Coaches should continue to enforce these truths throughout the season. Why? Because these traits—discipline, commitment, sacrifice, and continuing effort—are the same characteristics they will need to be successful in life.

Think back on your own life and remember those people who contributed to building and strengthening your character. What did the people see in you that no one else seemed to see? What lessons did they teach you? It may be that they taught you the importance of hard work, how to finish what you started, or something else. Sports provide countless situations where teaching and molding of strong character can take place, and these opportunities are invaluable to your players and to you. Having character traits such as a good attitude is key for everyone. Helping kids to have better attitudes, however, is the trick.

The challenge for coaches is to help players see the positives in life and to help them have a positive attitude, as the following story demonstrates. A young ballplayer went into his backyard with a bat and a ball and said, "I am the greatest hitter of all time!" He threw a ball up to himself and took a mighty swing. He missed. He picked up the ball and said, "I am the greatest hitter of all time, I am Hank Aaron," and threw the ball up in the air. He swung and missed again. One last time he exclaimed, "I am Babe Ruth and Mickey Mantle," and with a determined look on his face he tossed the ball in the air and swung a mighty blow. Nothing. The ball fell to the ground. The young player picked up the ball, put his bat over his shoulder, and started to leave the backyard, dejected. Then he said boldly, "Hey, I guess I am the greatest pitcher of all time."

As a coach, you are faced with invaluable opportunities every day, and if you deal with them correctly, the lessons you teach a player will last a lifetime. Then one day, if one of your players is asked the question, "Who helped mold your character?" I am sure he will say your name. The key is being sincere in your relationships with your players and always keeping your players best interests at heart.

Some lessons and character traits every student-athlete should be taught include:

- Honesty
- Fairness
- Teamwork
- Unselfishness

- Winning and losing with class
- Positive attitude
- Commitment
- Confidence
- Goal setting
- Determination
- Sharing
- Loyalty
- Respect
- Practice
- Choices
- Belonging
- Integrity
- Gratitude
- Sacrifice
- Pride

Of course, you can certainly add to this list, and you will know the character traits needed at the time—just like in your own case when you were young and someone pointed you in the right direction. The key is to recognize that the young person or other coach standing beside you needs your guidance and, in years to come, will appreciate your attention.

The question, of course, is how can coaches instill these types of important behaviors in the young athletes they coach year after year? And, if the coaches do not do it, who will? One coach told me she uses the "lesson-of-the-day" idea. She chooses the lesson of the day, which revolves around a character trait. If the coach chooses integrity, for instance, she has her coaches talk about integrity in several different situations as it applies to what the players are doing. Imagine all the lessons a player would learn in one day alone. Coaches do realize the importance of character with their students and players. Last year, I was asked to address this topic in the second half of a speech. The first part of the speech ran long and I asked the coaches if they really wanted to talk about character or continue with motivation. "Are you kidding us?" the coaches responded. "We definitely need to address this and could use all the help we can get. In many ways, it is our most challenging issue."

In 2002, the NFL Charities funded a study of 10 successful high school coaches, and once the study was completed, they provided recommendations for how to build character in athletes. The 10 coaches who participated all counted character-building as a top priority in their programs. Individually, they pointed out how they help build character through programs such as alternatives when cutting players or organizing a team-unity night each week. Specifically, as a group, they promoted:

- Having a relationship with their players by constantly communicating and emphasizing an open-door policy. You must have an open-door policy, so the student knows whether or not they can come to your office, and that you are available and care.

- Presenting clear expectations and holding players accountable for adherence to those expectations.

- Being flexible in dealing with individual players. One size does not fit all.

- Emphasizing individual player discipline.

- Emphasizing and instilling that each player understands their individual roles and the importance of teamwork.

- Emphasizing goal setting as well as having a success-oriented attitude.

- Practicing tough love (i.e., reprimanding player behavior, not personality) was emphasized by some of the coaches and tied to caring while holding players highly accountable for their actions. Charlie Johnston, the winningest high school football coach at one school in Texas, while at Childress High School said: "I had to really deal with each kid fairly and as an individual. I changed over the years. One way is I used to kick a player off for certain infractions; however, I realized if I did that I could have no influence over him and my opportunity to help him was done. I worked even harder to hold players accountable and to be responsible. but rarely did I show them the door."

- Serving as father figures, but not being seen as players' "buddies."

Additionally, most coaches know that each player and each situation is unique. However, they also know that the need to build character is the same, no matter the player's age, past experience, or the extent of their athletic talent and ability. The bottom line is: players need guidance and are starving for help.

Several years ago, I took 43 young people on a mission trip to the border of Mexico where we worked for Habitat for Humanity. On the way back home, we stopped at the Grand Canyon. Our plan was to camp and hike down 1.6 miles on one of the famous scenic trails, and we prepared for this strenuous trip by working out as a group and even going on a "trial trip" to the Palo Duro Canyon in West Texas. The day came and we hiked down. It was more than any of us could have ever expected—beautiful and vast. Even the kids were in awe, and you know how hard it is to find natural things that excite them. On the hike back up, several kids struggled. A distance of 1.6 miles may not sound like a difficult hike, but when it is almost straight up and with little air, it can be difficult—even for those who are in shape.

Two young ladies in the group found it difficult and had to stop several times. As a group, we should have waited with them, but the others had no idea they were behind and struggling. The three of us walked, stopped, sat down, fussed, and repeated this cycle several times. Every once in a while, they would say, "Eddie, I just can't make it. Call someone and have them come get us." We could have done that, and we surely would not have been the first or the last to call for help. Yet, we kept going, slowly and steadily.

Occasionally, I would say, "Oh, you'll make it. Keep going." Eventually, they did make it out, and as we stood on top of that incredible spot with a view that went on forever, catching our breaths, I told them to never forget how they made it and how they didn't give up. I told them I was proud of them and they should be proud of themselves.

As adults now, when difficult times arise, I hope they both remember back to that time in their young lives and what they achieved. I hope it makes them realize that no matter what life throws at them, they will make it and have the ability to reach the top. Building character can be difficult and yet so rewarding for everyone.

All They Want Is to Belong … and to Believe

"Let no one ever come to you without leaving better and happier."
                                                            —Mother Teresa

Mike Smith, a coach for more than 30 years, said in an interview that more than 80 percent of his athletes come from single-parent or single-adult homes. Many are being reared by their mothers, grandmothers, or other family members. In our coaching clinics, many coaches agree with these numbers and the ones who have players from two-parent families say that one or both parents are working to provide for their families and they are not always available, either.

When Coach Smith sits with his players at the beginning of each season, he begins seeing sparks as the team moves its focus to a single goal—to win ballgames and become champions in life. "They want to be part of something they enjoy," Smith explained. "They want to be able to relate, to build a bond, to have people respect what they're trying to achieve—and they want to believe."

How much do kids today want to believe? One coach put it this way, "Unlike kids 25 years ago, today's kids are savvy. They've seen heroes toppled from their pedestals. They see and hear much of what's good about our world, but they also are well aware of the underbelly of life. They know about parents who [mistreat] their kids…. They know kids who have parents in prison. They are well aware of many of life's realities, but if I, as a coach, can give them something to believe in, most of them focus in and embrace whatever it is." This "something" can be as simple as school or team traditions. Many teams traditionally touch a photograph, a banner or an old trophy before playing home games. It can be all about pride, reachable goals—or it can be about the other team."

Before a game against a team from the affluent side of town, Smith sat down with his players and told them their opponents that next Friday would be decked out in a lot of expensive equipment—equipment Smith's players couldn't afford. "They'll have on sweat bands, gloves, pads, and fancy shoes that we don't have," he explained. "Well, we don't need that stuff. We're good, and we can show them how good we are on Friday. By the way, you know why they're wearing that stuff? Because they know you're good and they're scared." His team believed—and played their hearts out and won.

Paul Kitagaki Jr. / Zuma Press

After working out his team for the next game, one coach reminded them of last year's meeting with the same team. "Remember how they disrespected our parents by making them sit on those sorry bleachers?" he asked. "Remember how they threw cups of ice at our band?" The players nodded. "This year when we play them, we want them to regret disrespecting anything about this school—and we'll do it on the playing field by giving 110 percent, making plays, and winning the game." The team was with him. They believed, and with that one spoken incentive, they pushed their daily practice effort to the next level and won the game.

Before the University of Texas–University of Southern California championship game for the 2005 season, some of the USC players told the media, "We're going to prove Vince Young didn't belong in New York as a Heisman Trophy nominee." They believed, and that was their focus, but the UT Longhorns were also focused, believing that they could prove them wrong. Of course, that wasn't their whole motivation, but USC's casting dispersions Young's way was one more hook Longhorn coaches could use to have the team believe the game really boiled down to a matter of pride and respect—and they won.

It is clear to me coaches really see the importance of teaching character. They know there are so many negative forces in the world, and they know kids need help. The problem is that progress is often slow; therefore, it is easy to get frustrated. Years ago, I was a camp counselor for young boys who had committed crimes. As counselors, we tried all kinds of things to get through to the boys a better and more positive way of carrying themselves. One thing we tried was to have the young men act out bible stories in an attempt to teach more responsible behavior. The problem was they seemed bored and didn't seem to care. After two nights, we abandoned this and let them do some other things. To my amazement, one of the toughest kids by far came up to me and asked "Hey, when are we going to do those bible stories again?" The lesson is: you never know. You just keep challenging, teaching, and being a good example.

6

Keeping It Fun

Darren McNamara / Getty Images Sport

After All, That's Why They Play

Statistics show, time and time again, the number-one reason student-athletes choose to play on any team is to have fun. While that may sound trite, it really is true. Of course, most good coaches would say, "Winning is fun!" However, if winning is the only thing emphasized, problems will begin to mount if the team suffers a loss or two.

Most student-athletes want fun options that keep the season fresh and exciting. The wear and tear of a season can definitely dilute the team's spirit and enthusiasm. Fun outings don't take a lot of time and can yield huge benefits. Invite the team to your school gym and let the fun begin. I have found that a little fun goes a long way, and an occasionally fun surprise pays huge dividends. This chapter includes many object-oriented lessons from coaches across the country. Try new things. The kids will love it, and you will teach lessons not soon forgotten. After all, when you consider the number of successful coaches who try different techniques and ideas and win, it may well worth it. What follows are some low-cost options. Keep in mind recreation really means re-creation. Recreation is fun and produces a new attitude and spirit.

> Tip: Have a contest where each coach heads up and develops a different event each month for the team. Then at the end of the season, give out dinner for two for the best event. You can also have seniors be responsible for planning and carrying out something fun.

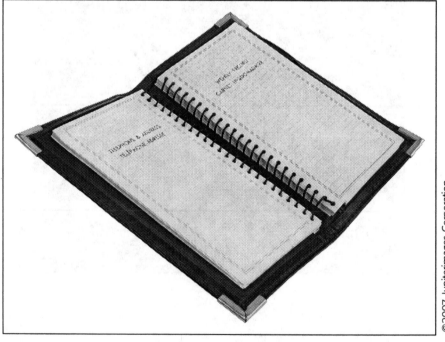

Team Nights

Monthly or weekly "team nights" will go a long way in building a true team. It is very important that everyone participates—all managers, trainers, players, and coaches. In the corporate world, Sam Walton wore a skirt at the New York Stock Exchange when they went public, and Herb Keller of Southwest Airlines has dressed like Elvis at stockholders meetings. Remember, they are always looking to you to set the tone. If you lead, the players and other coaches will follow. You will at least want to participate as a judge, referee, or the person handing out awards. Remember that the reason these events are so effective is players and coaches get the opportunity to laugh and see each other in a different light. It is also a great time to let kids be kids and to be "goofy" if they choose. You will have time to be serious on the playing field or court later. If the difference is clear between fun time and serious time, your players will know and respect the difference.

Scavenger Hunt—Amazing Race

Divide your team up into smaller teams (teams of five to eight work well). Take older or younger players and place them together. Let them come up with a team name. (What a great way to build teamwork!) Hide a list of objects around the campus. Give each team a list and a paper bag for the (usually) 25 objects to find or questions to answer. (Schools have all kinds of plaques or signs around them. No need to go into any building besides the gym, and no one may leave the campus.) Objects can range from a piece of paper to a question of what year the school was founded. They can also be challenges, like find a four-leaf clover, count the number of parking spaces, and answer trivia questions. Give points for each item. Have each team total up their points and meet back in one hour. Let the stories begin.

Crazy Olympics

Divide up your team in to groups of 8 to 10 and have a series of fun, crazy relays. Have someone make an Olympic-torch replica (usually out of tin foil) to start the games. Have the teams run into the gym with music playing. Points are given for first, second, and third of each relay. Relays range from:

- *Balloon Bust:* A player runs down with a partner from the team. One player blows up the balloon and the other pops it with his foot. They run back and tag the next group until everyone is finished. You can also have them bust the balloons on chairs.

- *Toilet-Paper Relay:* Line each team up single file behind each other. Take a roll of toilet paper and pass it under each player backwards. At the end, pass it back over their shoulder creating a human toilet-paper roll. Teams cannot throw or roll the paper as they pass it from one person to the next. The first team to unroll the paper wins. The idea is the all-the-way-under motion and then the all-the-way-over-the-top motion with the toilet paper until finished.

- *Hoops:* Get one large hoop (e.g., a Hula Hoop®) per team. Each person must run and pick up the hoop, then swing it around their hips at least five times before they can return to the team.

- *Plastic-Spoon Relay:* Give each person a spoon and a lifesaver. They must put the spoon in their mouth and run down with the lifesaver in the spoon. No hands are allowed, and if the player drops it, he or she must start over.

- *Human Mummy:* The team will surround one player and unroll the toilet paper roll as fast as possible around that person. The team who unrolls it first wins.

- *Crazy Eight:* Teams line up single file pointed toward a center object (usually a plastic trashcan, or a stand alone blocking dummy, something that can be knocked over.) The teams surround the object like spokes on a wagon wheel with teams in a circle facing the center. Players run toward and around the object one full turn. Then they run back to their team and tag the next person. The key is to go all the way around the object while everyone from the other teams does the same.

- *Banana Relay:* Teams line up single file, and each team is given a banana. The teams pass the banana down with their left hands and back up with their right to the last person who eats the banana. The team to have the banana eaten first wins.

- *Closing Ceremony:* While playing Olympic music, hand out medals or goofy prizes.

Movie Night

Many motivational sports movies would make for a great fun evening. Many of the movies that are considered "classics" were released before many of today's student-athletes were born. Different movies at different times may be perfect, depending on the team's needs. Have lots of popcorn, and be sure to check the movie ratings first:

- *Field of Dreams*
- *Hoosiers*
- *Remember the Titans*
- *Rocky (1976)*
- *The Natural*
- *Sea Biscuit*
- *Rudy*
- *Chariots of Fire*
- *Eight Men Out*
- *Miracle*
- *Tin Cup*
- *Road to Glory*

Bowling Night

Among the reasons why so many teams have a mini-bowling tournament for their teams: it's cheap, fun, and no one gets hurt. Rent out a local alley on a slow night, divide up the teams, and roll out the fun.

Winners Flag Competition and Team Chant

Give the team everything they need to make a team flag—including a pole, blank flag, felt, glue, and so forth. The team will design a flag based on the individual gifts each player brings to the table and the team spirit they have for their school and team. They will also develop a team chant or song to show their team spirit.

Build Your Own Putt-Putt Competition

Divide your team into smaller groups. Each group is given all the objects needed to make individual holes (PVC pipe or rope, wood, golf balls, and clubs). Each hole can have its own theme—from "Groovy '70s" to "Western," you name it. Points will be given for creativity, and then the players play the course, putting alternate style. Alternate shot means each person on the team hits the ball only one time until it is holed passing the putters to their teammates between shots. Total the number of putts for all the holes and award winners. This event can be held in the gym, especially if you use Styrofoam balls as golf balls, which work great on a slick gym floor.

Build Your Own Rocket Ship Competition

Give each team a rocket-ship kit (Estes® rocket ships can be purchased for about $16.00 each from most large national retail outlets) that they will put together. Groups can usually do this activity in about 15 to 20 minutes, and they love the challenge. Place a target on the ground in the middle of the football field. Have the team launch their rocket in the air, trying to land the ship as close to the target as possible. Award points for first up and closest to the target.

Game-Film Night

The coach sets a game film to fun music and invites the team to come and watch. Of course, later they dissect the film, but on this night, it's pure fun—especially if their team won.

To keep practices fun, remember the reasons players play: to have fun, to be on a team, and to compete. Set up as many competitions as possible: two-on-two drills, free-throw contests, get the coach in the goal for hockey, let others try to kick field goals, and so on. These competitions do not get in the way of your teachable times. They simply add an element of fun for everyone. When you see a moment that is appropriate for a break in the action, add an element of creativity and watch everyone's excitement.

> "You can learn more about a person in one hour of play than a year of conversation."
>
> —Plato

7

How to Build a True Home-Field Advantage

Richard Du Bois

Motivating Parents and Boosters

Everyone in sports understands the importance of a true home-field advantage. An important question is: how can you get parents, boosters, and others involved in supporting your team? Keep in mind, boosters and regular fans are not the same thing. Boosters make a commitment to a team. Boosters can be a great asset to your coaching staff. You have never heard of a "fair-weather booster," have you? In this day and age, if you want the ability to purchase or invest in more than your current athletic budget might allow, you need all the help you can get. After all, if you cultivate good boosters and get enthused parents on your side, you can spend your time coaching. Remember: you are in the people business, and parents and boosters are part of "your" people.

It seems that all coaches at every level have had to (and will forever have to) deal with parents and boosters. Whether you are coaching pee-wee or professional ball, parents and booster-club members will be a part of your team. From the screaming parent of a four-year-old soccer player to Donovan McNabb's mother butting into the locker room making sure the players eat their soup, if you coach for even one season, you will see them all. At times, boosters can be as annoying at flees on a dog, and yet there are other times when they help out in incredible ways. Parents and boosters can be a real asset to your team or they can be a liability. Parents and boosters can eat up your time. Both can alienate players and the community—basically making your life very difficult.

Of course, parents can also be a great source of support and encouragement. Properly motivated, both can be a positive part of the team atmosphere. For the most part, parents' and boosters' levels of involvement fall into one of three categories: too much, too little, and just right. Obviously, what all coaches are after is the "just right." For many coaches, "too little" involvement does not exist. No coach wants others interfering with his ability to coach. Coaches do not need the input of a parent to help draw up plays or decide on a starting lineup. As long as a coach's patience holds up, he will generally do his best to humor parents by fielding their questions and nodding his head at their suggestions. However, from all the coaches we interviewed, we learned that this behavior can only go on so long before something bad happens, as demonstrated by the following story.

> "There is nothing wrong with the Little League World Series that locking out the adults couldn't cure."
>
> — Mike Penner, a writer from Los Angeles

In the beginning of the third quarter of a high school football game in northern Arkansas, a time-out was called by the home team to make sure the defense was ready for a big third-down play. Later in that same quarter, some confusion occurred on the offensive side and the home team called a second time-out. Soon after that, a third (and last) time-out was called. As it turned out, the team could have really used those time-outs. Down by a touchdown, they got the ball back with less than a minute to play. With no time-outs, they fell just short of driving the field and scoring the winning touchdown.

After the game, a player's father approached one of the assistant coaches, and in a rather benign and friendly manner, asked a rather ridiculous question, "Coach, why didn't you guys try to save your time-outs for when you really needed them?" The coach exploded and retorted, "If you don't like the way we call a game, you can take your son and go play some place else!" The father was, of course, offended by the harsh reply. He immediately, in a crowd of other parents, shared what the coach had said and by that night the parents (who were also suffering from another frustrating, close loss) were talking amongst themselves about what a lousy group of coaches they had. The parents were in a sense poisoning the community against the team.

How harsh were the coach's words? How unreasonable can parents be? At the end of the year, the offended dad took his 6'6" all-district linebacker and transferred out of the district. No apology from any or all of the coaches could erase that one moment of humiliation and disrespect. (Never underestimate a parent's sense of family pride—once offended is often once too many.)

Was the father out of line? Was the coach out of line? Yes, of course, for both parties. To some extent both parties were out of line. An *informed* parent or booster would never approach a coach immediately after losing a close game. An *informed* parent or booster would realize that immediately after a game, the coaches and players are both still emotionally charged. Yes, because even an emotionally-charged coach needs to dig deep, bite his lip, and keep moving. An ancient proverb is used amongst those who teach the martial arts: "One moment of patience will save you 100 hours of sorrow." At team UP, Inc., we work with parents and boosters to remind them of the positive role they can play.

After a session with managers and owners of small charter companies, I had an owner tell me of a serious mistake he made with a longtime, cantankerous customer. He said, "The customer had been so out of line, I just couldn't take it anymore. The customer began complaining, and in a fit of frustration I told the customer exactly what I really thought of him. It wasn't pretty. I was so frustrated, and it had built up for a long time. The customer's reply was simply, "Okay." He then promptly moved his plane from my company, as did two of his friends. The three planes accounted for 35 percent of my business. To make it worse, every day I still get to watch those planes take off and land, only now they use a different company. I wish I had handled it differently."

The reality is that the relationship between coaches and parents does not have to be adversarial, either. If proper steps are taken, everyone can be on the same team and enjoy success together. Being proactive with parents and boosters is the key and will keep you from having to be reactive later. When you are proactive, you are in charge. When you are reactive, the situation is often in charge. Also, remember: if you lose your temper with a parent or booster, you lose. After all, when you lose your temper, you can't think as well as usual, and it sends the wrong message to everyone.

At *Team Up*, we teach three things to remember when dealing with parents and boosters at any level. In a proactive manner, keep everyone:

- Informed
- Involved
- Intrigued

Informed

Good communication with parents and boosters can be the difference between an enjoyable season and a miserable one. The sooner the channels of communication open between you and them, the better. No matter what your past experiences have been with parents or boosters or what you might think about them—you *need* them. They are the ones who will get your players up early for practice and will come late to pick them up after practice. They are the ones who will sell cookies or buy the team a scoreboard when needed. They will also put out fires behind your back. Remember the old adage: "Give them what they want and need and you will get what you want and need." Parents and boosters want to be informed and to be able to help the team. It takes extra as the coaching staff to accommodate them, but you can also reap huge rewards.

Our research shows that the number-one concern of parents during the season is communication. Parents often feel out of the loop when it comes to their child's participation in school athletics. Adolescents/young adults are not known for their ability to transfer or disseminate information. What is told to them at 4:00 in the afternoon may very well be gone from their minds by 4:02.

> "The biggest miscommunication is to assume communication has taken place."
> —Unknown

Parents' Meeting

The one most important thing you can do—no matter how big or small your program—is to have a pre-season parents' meeting. This meeting can take place after a pride night or it can be a stand-alone event. It can be a big deal with the booster club also being invited to participate by providing refreshments and then allow them to sit and hear your comments. This meeting might be your one chance to sell yourself and your program to the parents, and it is also your opportunity to motivate them! You probably meet regularly with booster members. If not, start now. A parents or boosters' meeting before the season may save you a season's worth of conflict.

Old-school coaches may think parents' meetings are a waste of time. However, 21st-century parents are a different breed than those of 30 or 40 years ago. Forty years ago, parents didn't send their kids to sports camps or spend money for personal trainers or participate on traveling teams. Times are different, and today parents want to be informed. They will come to your pre-season meeting. At the parents' meeting, you will be able to:

- Give out pertinent information, such as practice schedules, game day routines, and so forth.
- Lay out the expectations of the team and of the parents.
- Lay out team rules.
- Inform the parents when you are available to talk with them. This point is important! Have a set time when you will be available to visit with parents. That time is not right before practice or right after practice. It is not on game day—period! Boosters will also overhear this and heed the information.

Web Page

If your school has a web page, use it. If your school does not have a website, then get one. Keep team information on the page and keep it updated. Doing so will save you hours of grief in dealing with parents and boosters. A web site is a great way to keep the parents both informed and intrigued.

Be selective advertising your email address. It is too easy to be confrontational via e-mail. E-mail also requires a response. If you are the personality type that takes a while to respond, you will only add fuel to a possibly already volatile situation. If a parent or booster is upset with you for any reason, you want them to have to come to you at your convenience and speak to you face to face. Remember: their concerns may be valid; no coach is beyond reproach. Nonetheless, it is always to your advantage to play on your home court/office. To keep parents and boosters informed:

- Schedule a pre-season parents' meeting hosted by the booster club.
- Maintain a school web page with game schedules and times.
- Insist on consistency from the coaching staff, which generally means starting and ending practice on time. Parents do not like to wait any more than you do.

Involved

Some parents will want to be involved and some will not. Both types of parents are a concern. Properly involving parents in your season will be of great benefit to you and your team. Your goal is to help the parents understand they, too, are part of the team. You must let them know what position you want them to play. Not all parents will participate; however, if your staff makes the effort to communicate, parents will generally respond.

Pre-Season

A father-son or mother-daughter retreat can accomplish many things. It will bond your team and help build relationships between coaches and parents. The coaches can also host a dinner with fathers and/or mothers. If a parent cannot attend an event for any reason, a booster can "stand in" as a supporter for the player.

During the Season

- Invite parents and boosters to pep rallies. Most will be working, but at least they have been invited and included.
- At a basketball game or football game, have the parents form the spirit line on the court/field for the players run through and high five at the beginning of the game.
- Have the booster club do a weekly drawing and allow one parent to be the honorary coach that week. Have them travel with the team and eat the pre-game meal with the team. Allow them to be on the field during warm-ups and on the bench during the game. After a parent has experienced being the honorary coach, he will never look at your program the same.

Intrigued

Keeping parents intrigued is important to keeping their enthusiasm elevated. The bottom line is that parents want what is best for their child. If being on your team is benefiting their child, chances are they are going to do whatever they can to help you. Parents who are properly intrigued will run through a brick wall for you if they think their child is benefiting from your program.

High school and junior high student-athletes are more likely to listen to a coach than to a parent. The parents know this. A coach encouraging a student-athlete to work harder in school carries more weight than if mom or dad tells him. Keep parents intrigued by letting them you can have their child's full attention anytime you want it. Also, keep information on your website such as: kids who participate in school athletics are less likely to drop out of school. Promote responsibility, greater academic success, an appreciation of personal health and fitness and strong social bonds.

Parents need to hear about their child's potential. They need to hear about how students who participate on athletic teams are more likely to succeed in the "real" world. If you want to have a true home-field advantage, show you care all the time. At Team Up, we provide sessions for parents and boosters for many teams. Most times, they simply want to be informed and want to be an asset. They simply need to be given boundaries and expectations, just like anyone else.

©2007 Jupiterimages Corporation

Reaching Out to the Community

Volunteer Projects

Another great way to create a true home-field advantage is to volunteer in the community. Call Habitat for Humanity or another local charity and let them know you have a heck of a workforce willing to help on a project. Nothing helps bring a team together more than helping someone else—and the good press can't hurt in the community.

Civic Organization Speeches

An important part of the coaching job is to speak to community groups. Civic organizations such as Rotary, Kiwanis, Optimists, Civitans, and others are always looking for speakers to present programs at their weekly meetings. Coaches are always welcomed speakers. If you have not been invited to speak to these groups, then speak with your principal or school superintendent. Chances are they belong to one of these organizations. Speaking to these groups will go a long way in developing community support for your team and for your coaching tenure. A few things to remember about civic groups include:

- These groups consist of professional people who have a vested interest in the community and in your school.

- These groups are not your players. Do not treat them as such.

- These groups will usually conduct their meeting around a meal. Most likely it will be lunch. However, you may be asked to speak at a breakfast or dinner meeting.

- Because your audience will have to get to work, you will have a limited time to speak. Make sure you know exactly how long you have, and leave time for a Q&A session.

- Civic group meetings are usually less than exciting, so this opportunity will be a chance for you to impress.

- These groups will be very interested in hearing what you have to say. You will have their attention from the time you are introduced. Your job is to keep their attention.

Remember: the people in these organizations are community leaders. They are interested in knowing what you are doing to develop future community leaders. The civic groups will want to hear two things from you:

- What are you doing for their community?

- What is going on with your team?

Sample Speech

Thank you very much for having me today. I have heard great things about your club and I hope you have heard great things about our program.

You may have heard the story* involving Yogi Berra, the well-known catcher for the New York Yankees, and Hank Aaron, who at that time was the chief power hitter for the Milwaukee Braves. The teams were playing in the World Series, and as usual Yogi was keeping up his ceaseless chatter, intended to pep up his teammates on one hand and to distract the Milwaukee batters on the other. As Aaron came to the plate, Yogi tried to distract him by saying, "Henry, you're holding the bat wrong. You're supposed to hold it so you can read the trademark." Aaron didn't say anything, but when the next pitch came, he hit it into the left-field bleachers. After rounding the bases and tagging up at home plate, Aaron looked at Yogi Berra and said, "I didn't come up here to read."

People often think that coaches are here just to win, and believe me, we feel the pressure to win. If we didn't want to win, if we weren't competitive, we probably wouldn't have decided to go into coaching. Winning is something that will take care of itself if we take care of the other things.

Hank Aaron came to the plate to hit; I came to coach. Coaching means much more than just trying to win games. It also encompasses preparation and discipline and trying to mold these young people into respectable citizens.

A recent survey found that 20 percent of all teenagers think that one day they will be famous—and many of our ballplayers think the same, so we don't want to squash that dream. We want to use that dream to drive them to improve. However, reality says that many of them will not be famous and most of them will not make a living playing ball. Let me share some statistics with you. These stats come from the NCAA website, www.ncaa.org:

- 2.9 percent of high school senior boys playing on the basketball team will play at an NCAA member institution, and 0.03 percent will eventually get drafted by an NBA team. That's 3 in 10,000.

- 3.1 percent of high school senior girls playing on the basketball team will play at an NCAA member institution, and 0.02 percent of will eventually get drafted by a WNBA team. That's 1 in 5,000.

- 5.58 percent of high school boys playing on the football team will to on to play at an NCAA member institution, and 0.09 percent will be drafted by an NFL team. That's 9 in 10,000.

*J. M. Boice, *Learning to Lead*, Revell, 1990, p. 38.

- 5.6 percent of high school senior boys playing on the baseball team will go on to play at an NCAA member institution, and 0.5 percent will eventually be drafted by a MLB team. That's 25 in 5,000.

We very well may have players who will go on to play at the next level, and we may even have a player who will one day play professionally. However, because of the numbers I just shared with you, we as a coaching staff are not just interested in victories on the field or the court, but our coaching staff is also interested in victories off the field or the court. It is our job to make sure they are ready for the world in case a scholarship is not in their future. Let me say this again: we want to win on the field, but we also want to win off the field. Now having said all of that, I want to share with you what is going on with our team."

[Do not spend too much time talking about your star players. Instead, talk about the team and team goals. Talk about expectations. Emphasize your desire for each player to improve. Be very careful about making predictions about wins or loses. Never speak negatively about other teams, players, or coaches.]

Harry S. Truman once gave a speech in which he said, "I remember an epitaph which is in the cemetery at Tombstone, Arizona. It says, 'Here lies Jack Williams. He done his damnedest. I think that is the greatest epitaph a man can have. When a man gives everything that is in him to do the job he has before him, that is all you can ask of him and that is what I have tried to do.'"

As the coach, I am just trying to do my damnedest. I am just trying to do my best—and my best will be measured by whether I can get the best out of my players, if I can get the best out of our student body and out of our parents and out of our community. We want to win games, and I fully go into every game playing to win. But the long-term benefit to this community will come if we can help build better citizens and future leaders. If every player, coach and person in the stands can say that they gave their best, then we will always leave the field/court with our heads held high.

Again, thank you for having me today. I want to encourage all of you to come out and watch us play. Every game is a big game, and your presence in the stands does make a difference. I want to encourage you to pat our players on the back when you see them around town. Let me close with these words from the great Knute Rockne. He said, "Success is never final and failure is never fatal. It is courage that counts. That courage is what we hope we are teaching our players."

8

Giving True Recognition That Works

See It, Say It!

If you have a large number of players on your team, you know it is impossible to spend a significant about of time with each player. A football coach will only encounter each player individually for about 20 seconds a day. Of course, the standout players will usually get more of your attention, and chances are these players are already highly motivated. A question to ponder is: how do you spend your 20 seconds with the rest of the players? Are the encounters positive or negative? What do you say or do?

> "People will forget what you said, but people will never forget how you made them feel."
>
> —Lee Colan

© Rich Kane/USP/ZUMA Press

Tip: Make the player either feel appreciated or teach them something with each encounter.

If you take the time to teach or correct the players, it means they matter to you. If they didn't matter, you would not take the time—and nothing is worse than when you are on the team and the coach doesn't miss you if you miss practice. You can make each encounter positive by either saying something constructive about what you saw or teaching your players a better way.

"Perhaps once in 100 years, a person may be ruined by excessive praise, but surely once every minute someone dies from a lack of it."

—Unknown

Justin Kase Conder / Zuma Press

Kevin Reece / Icon SMI / Zuma Press

Tip: Make each 20-second encounter motivating.

William James, the father of psychology, said human beings have a fundamental need to be appreciated, and in the end, people simply do more for those who appreciate them. People don't mind being held accountable when they know their ideas and actions are appreciated. When players feel like their effort is appreciated, their effort surges to unbelievable levels. At that point, you are able to answer the question, "How did he get so much out of that team?"

Most coaches feel they are much more appreciative than the players think they are. Sometimes coaches intend to tell the players or other coaches what a great job they did, but they never get around to it. The problem is that too many coaches make the mistake of *thinking* their players know the coach respects and appreciates them. Just because you—as the coach—think something good about the player does not mean they know you think that. You must tell them.

One issue players have (and one of the main reasons players say they quit) is they feel coaches place too much emphasis on too few players. Think about five players to whom you say something all the time. Think of five players you need to speak to more. Think of 10 players you need to spend time with that need your help. Remember that the players you pass off to an assistant coach will likely become key players in the future. Start working with those players—do not wait.

When you see a player doing something good, tell him. It's that simple. No one is going to think you are too nice, they will think you appreciate their effort and will work harder.

Tips for Giving Recognition that Works

- Make the recognition specific. Tell the player what they are doing well.

- Share the credit. Gene Stallings said Bear Bryant was great at sharing the credit and it made all the coaches and players work harder.

- If you give out an MVP award at your banquet, make sure the player knows to give credit to others. At the banquet, you can remind everyone that a great college coach at his team's year-end banquet said the following about his All-American: "Johnny is a great player, and a fine young man. He throws the ball with great accuracy. He is a team leader. Truthfully, there is only one problem with him, he is a graduating senior."

- Hand out other awards, especially character recognition awards, at the banquet that will mean something to everyone. Some examples include: the Mr. Hustle Award, the True Sacrifice Award, and the Comeback Player of the Year. Think in terms of the message you send to others sitting there for next season.

- Provide effort stickers for players' helmets. Some coaches are wary of using stickers to reward individual effort because it can be counterproductive to the rest of the team if it's not handled well. When used correctly, however, helmet stickers can provide a great message to everyone about team effort and success. For example, Brad Fichtel—a coach from Rockwall, Texas ISD and former player for the St. Louis Rams—gives a helmet sticker to *every* player on the field when a player scores or makes a great play.

- Give "practice" balls to players. Game balls have been a great source of motivation for years. Why not give them for practice? You don't have to give out expensive leather balls every time. Buy some cheaper balls and give them to players who give that extra effort. It's the thought that counts and these gestures can go a long way in motivating players.

- Make it extremely special the first time a player is able to wear your school's logo—including practice and a game. Make it an honor to wear your team's uniform and make sure they understand your tradition. Invite in those players who went before them to tell of the heritage they continue.

"Soldiers will die in battle for a ribbon."

—Napoleon

What About the Bench Players?

> "Recognize everyone's gifts and talents. After all, it's not who starts the game, it's who finishes."
>
> —John Wooden

Coaches win with players. Everybody knows that. No one will criticize a coach for playing players who give the team the best chance to win. The competency of any coach at any level might very well fall into question if he didn't. The coach makes sure the starters are prepared and motivated to play hard. After all, Bear Bryant said, "Get your best players in the game, not on the sideline." But what about the bench player?

I recently attended a junior high (ninth grade) basketball game between two very good teams. I was told these were two of the best teams in the state. Sure enough, I was not disappointed. Both teams possessed a collection of players with skills well beyond their years.

The crowd in the gym was standing room only. This contest was a big game. As the game wore on, I noticed that the Spurs substituted players regularly. In fact, in the first half alone, 10 players were sent into the game. The Bulls, on the other hand, substituted one player one time the entire first half.

In the second half, the lead went back and forth. In the middle of the fourth quarter, the outcome was still very much in doubt. Then, in the blink of an eye, something happened that dictated the outcome. The Bulls lost a player with a turned ankle. The coach quickly substituted another player and the game continued. Then, the Bulls lost another player with five personal fouls.

As I watched the Bulls' coach, I could see from the look in his eyes that the game was over. As I watched the Spurs' coach, I could see that he, too, realized he had just been the recipient of a great gift—an unprepared coach. Needing to substitute in another player, the Bulls' coach stood scanning his bench reserves with no idea who to put into the game. His four remaining players stood on the floor, out of breath and waiting for him to choose a player. The referee, the crowd, and the opposing coach stood waiting—all of them with their eyes on a coach who had a look of dismay on his face. Advantage Spurs.

The body language of the Bulls' coach told everyone in the gym—including the opposing coach—that he was not prepared for what had just happened, nor had he prepared his players. As the coach stood scanning his bench, I looked at his players. All of them were looking at their shoes. None was making eye contact with the coach. Their body language told everyone in the gym that they were not eager or prepared to go into the game. At that time, I am not sure any of them wanted to go in.

A close game turned quickly into a cakewalk. At the urging of the referee, the Bulls' coach finally chose a player. Sixty seconds later, he substituted with another player in that same position. The next time out, he substituted that player. The opposing coach, sensing the uncertainty of the situation, turned on the heat. He pressed the Bulls into three straight turnovers: game over.

It was obvious that the bench players had not come to the game prepared to play. It was obvious that the coach had no confidence in them, and thus they had no confidence in themselves. A team is a reflection of its coach. If he is confident, the team will be confident. If he is not confident, the team will not be confident. The Bulls' coach could have learned something from Bill Yeoman when he said, "The single most important thing in motivation is the chance to succeed through hard work. You tell your kids to work hard, and I don't care if it's the fifth teamer, there has to be a reward for them. You have to move him up, get him on a trip or on special teams." It takes more than five players to make a winning team. The starting five may win a game, but it takes the whole team to win a championship.

Players must be watching, waiting, and hoping—sometimes agonizingly—for that chance to use his special skill to better the team. He may be just the one fast enough to break the press that has been killing the team or the tall player who can go in and stop an overactive center no one else can seem to keep off the boards. It may be a player from the bench who demonstrates to the fans that this team really has character and is willing to do whatever it takes to win—even sacrifice their glory. More importantly, it may be the whole bench that starters look to late in the game when they are hurting, out of breath, and burning inside for that spirit, that push, that enthusiasm, and that love necessary to make the big play and win for the whole team. In the end, bench players truly are one turned ankle away from being in the papers for either something good or bad. Like John Wooden said, "In the end, it's not who starts the game anyway. It's who finishes."

Make sure your bench players show up prepared to play, not prepared to sit. Spend as much time motivating them and preparing them for a game as you do your starters. Ensure that your players understand how close they are to being in the game and

> "Every coach will have some money players, but you have to keep things in perspective. Each individual has to understand that without the other members of team, there's no chance for success. It's often difficult to keep the super players from getting carried away with publicity, so the coach has to help them realize they're not the reason for the season. They're not the only players."
>
> —Ed Lehnick, former football head coach and Amarillo ISD athletic director

making a huge impact. Be aware of the messages you send with your body language to your players. Make sure they realize how much you respect their hard work and commitment. Coach Robert Hughes, the winningest high school basketball coach in Texas, said, "I prepare all 11 players to play in the game, and they know they will play. They are ready at any point, and it has made a huge difference in our success."

"Coaches must instill in their players a sense that they do have the opportunity to make a difference in the game at any moment."

—Shane Dreiling

Randall Benton / Zuma Press

Motivation Through Body Language

Think about not only *what* you say, but *how* you say it. Whether addressing a player or an entire team, the words you choose are crucial. More important may be the way in which you deliver those words. Are your words consistent with how you are delivering the message? If you want to be an effective communicator (and especially an effective and consistent motivator), you will need to be aware of both the words you speak and *how* you speak them.

Dr. Albert Mehrabian is known for having done groundbreaking research on communication. He became known for his work on the importance of both verbal and non-verbal communication. Dr. Mehrabian preaches the 7/38/55 percent rule of communication. His studies conclude that three elements are crucial in any face-to-face communication, and each of the three elements accounts differently for the meaning of the message:

- Words (7 percent of the message)
- Tone of voice (38 percent of the message)
- Body language (55 percent of the message)

Players are listening to your words, but not nearly as much as they are listening to the tone of your voice and your body language. A message becomes confusing if your words are saying one thing and your tone or body language is saying another. For effective and meaningful communication, these three parts of the message need to support each other in meaning. If they do not agree, your message may fall short of its intended effectiveness.

Consider the following example: You are in the locker room before a game. You and the team both know that your opponent will be formidable. Deep down inside you have your doubts about your team's chances. Reality says you will have to play your best and create some breaks if you are going to win the game. You address your team:

- Verbal: "We have worked hard, and I believe we can win if we just stick to our game plan and keep our heads high."
- Non-Verbal: Little eye contact with players, closed or slumped body posture, passionless tone of voice, worry in your face.

This example may be an exaggeration, but the point is that it is more likely that the team will accept the predominant form of communication, which according to Dr. Mehrabian's findings is non-verbal, 38 percent plus 55 percent. The literal meaning of the words is only 7 percent of the message and will only be processed by the players after the tone of your voice and your body language. Remember, they *hear* you, but more importantly, they also *see* you. Consider the difference in the following example:

- Verbal: "We have worked hard, and I believe we can win this game if we will stick to our game plan and keep our heads high!"
- Non-Verbal: Eye contact with as many of the players as possible, open posture, finger pointing at the players and to the field or court, passion in your voice, and a fearless look on your face.

The players have just heard the same words, but they certainly did not hear the same message. To motivate players, you must give recognition and make sure your body language matches your words. Young people and communities are looking for leaders and will follow if your message is positive, thought out, and consistent. Coach Javier Navarrete from Brownville ISD says he teaches his players to be positive no matter what the situation and to show their enthusiasm.

Remember to Recognize

In their book, *The Carrot Principal*, Adrian Gostick and Chester Elton note that 79 percent of employees who quit their jobs cite a lack of recognition as a key reason for leaving.* They also reveal that 65 percent of Americans received no praise or recognition in the workplace in the past year. Gostick and Elton draw the conclusion that if you want to get the most out of your employees, they need to know they matter. Furthermore, they report that once people realize they matter to the company, those people become more committed, loyal, and hard working.

Your players are no different. They need to know they matter. They need to know you notice what they are doing. Coaches who regularly recognize players (individually) report increased effort and overall improved attitudes.

Coach Ronnie Peacock at Rogers High School in Rogers, Arkansas, told us about what he calls Praise Day. Unbeknownst to his players, he has each of his coaches choose a player. During practice that day, each coach pays extra attention to his chosen player. They make sure to praise the player and to pat him on the back and to call him by name. The coach makes sure his particular player knows he is noticed and appreciated. At the next Praise Day, the coaches choose a new group of players to praise. Praise Day can be done periodically or it can be done at every practice.

Most of us are quick to notice when a player does something wrong. Remember to recognize when they do things right. Remembering to recognize will pay great dividends for you and for your team.

*Adrian Gostick and Chester Elton, *The Carrot Principal*, Free Press: New York, 2007. p. 8.

9

Motivational Tools: Quotes, Speeches, Stories, and Jokes

Rick Scuteri / Zuma Press

Quotes

Character

"Know how to win and how to lose and be able to handle adversity."
—Tom Osborne

"Look for players with character and ability. But remember, character comes first."
—Joe Gibbs

"We are what we repeatedly do. Excellence, then, is not an act, but a habit."
—Aristotle

"Be more concerned with your character than with your reputation, because your character is what you really are, while your reputation is merely what others think you are."
—Knute Rockne

"You win with good people. Character is just as important as ability."
—Don Shula

"I have tried to teach them to show class, to have pride and to display character. I think football, winning games, takes care of itself if you do that."
—Bear Bryant

"Your behavior is a reflection of what you truly believe."
—Hyrum W. Smith

"Small deeds done are better than great deeds planned."
—Peter Marshall

"Men do not attract that which they want, but that which they are."
—James Allen

"The biggest mistake coaches make is taking borderline cases and trying to save them. I'm not talking about grades. I'm talking about character. I want to know before a boy enrolls about his home life and what his parents want him to be."
—Bear Bryant

"People are eternally divided into two classes: the believer, builder, and praiser, and the unbeliever, destroyer, and critic."
—John Ruskin

Courage

"Courage means being afraid to do something, but still doing it."
—Knute Rockne

"'I can't' are words that have never been in my vocabulary."
—Wilma Rudolph

"Success is never final and failure is never fatal. It is courage that counts."
—Knute Rockne

Praise

"You can motivate players better with kind words than you can with a whip."
—Bud Wilkerson

"Be liberal in your praise; it costs nothing and it encourages much."
—Horace Mann

"I think we ought to impress on both our girls and boys that successful marriages require just as much work, just as much intelligence and just as much unselfish devotion, as they give to any position they undertake to fill on a paid basis."
—Eleanor Roosevelt, March 28, 1941

"Praise loudly. Criticize softly."
—Lou Holtz

"Inspire and motivate your players with praise. Ten years from now, it won't matter what your record was. What matters is this: Will your kids love you or hate you?"
—Jim Harrick

Encouragement

"Do the very best you can with what you have."
—Theodore Roosevelt

"Excellence is doing a common thing in an uncommon way."
—Booker T. Washington

"If you don't have the best of everything, make the best of everything you have."
—Erik Russell

"It is never too late to be what you might have been."
—George Eliot

"Never discourage anyone who continually makes progress, no matter how slow."
—Plato

Preparation

"It's not the will to win that matters. Everyone has that.
It's the will to prepare that matters."
—Bear Bryant

"We kept fighting and it paid off in the end. We had a phenomenal day,
and it was nice to see these ladies win the title they deserved all along."
—Bev Kearney, coach, University of
Texas women's track after winning Big
12 indoor title in 2006

Confidence

"We tend to get what we expect."
—Norman Vincent Peale

"Human beings can alter their lives by altering their attitudes of mind."
—William James

"Winner or losers are not born; they are the product of how they think."
—Lou Holtz

"When it gets right down to the wood-chopping, the
key to winning is confidence."
—Darrell Royal

"Winning isn't getting ahead of others. It's getting ahead of yourself."
—Roger Staubach

"In reading the lives of great men, I found that the
first victory they won was over themselves."
—Harry S Truman

"In order to win, you must expect to win.
You might even call it the arrogance factor."
—Dan Fouts

"Confidence is preparation's twin."
—Michael S. Clouse

"Always remember that Goliath was a 40-point favorite over Little David."
—Shug Jordan, Auburn coach

"Your mind believes what you tell it."
—Paul J. Meyer

"Knowing where you're going is the first step to getting there."
—Ken Blanchard

Perseverance

"Fall down seven times. Stand up eight."
—Japanese proverb

"I will prepare, and someday my chance will come."
—Abraham Lincoln

"Success is the sum of small efforts repeated day in and day out."
—Robert Collier

"Pray not for a lighter load, but for stronger shoulders."
—Unknown

"Winners never quit, and quitters never win."
—Vince Lombardi

"Two frogs fell into a bowl of cream. One didn't panic. Instead, he relaxed and drowned. The other kicked and struggled so much that the cream turned to butter and he walked out."
—Unknown

Positive Attitude

"I think the most important thing of all for any team is a winning attitude. The coaches must have it. The players must have it. The student body must have it. If you have dedicated players who believe in themselves, you don't need a lot of talent."
—Bear Bryant

"You cannot change what happens to you. You can only change how you will respond to what happens."
—Unknown

"What song do you have playing inside of you? Is it a positive, upbeat melody or something different? The reality is people can hear it coming from you all the time."
—Eddie Hill

"Don't listen to 'Ah, nah' people. You know what I mean—people who say, 'Ah, nah. You can't do this,' or 'Ah, nah. You can't do that.' Instead, listen to the 'Oh, yeah' people. They are the ones who get it done!"
—Eddie Hill

"The most important thing is team morale."
—Dean Smith

"I'm not the best, I just wanted it more."
—Bruce Jenner

"Your attitude reflects your altitude."
—Jim Alfonso

"I will not let anything get in the way of me and my competitive enthusiasm to win."
—Michael Jordan

"If you practice with emotion and purpose, you'll play with passion and confidence."
—Unknown

"The hitchhiker who sucks his thumb never gets anywhere."
—Unknown

Perspective

"The main thing is getting people to play. When you think it's your system that's winning, you're in for a damn big surprise"
—Burn Phillips

"The essence of sports is that while you're doing it, nothing else matters, but after you stop, there is a place, generally not very important, where you would put it."
—Roger Bannister

"We work to become, not to acquire."
—Elbert Hubbard

"Victories come about by simplicity, not complexity; by solidity, not experimentation; by dedication, not imagination."
—Woody Hayes

"I will not accept anything less than the best a player's capable of doing, and he has the right to expect the best that I can do for him and the team."
—Lou Holtz

"People don't care how much you know until they know how much you care."
—Lou Holtz

"It's easy to have faith in yourself and have discipline when you're a winner, when you're number one. What you've got to have is faith and discipline when you're not yet a winner"
—Vince Lombardi

"The price of success is hard work, dedication to the job at hand, and the determination that whether we win or lose, we have applied the best of ourselves to the task at hand."
—Vince Lombardi

"Certainly a leader needs a clear vision of the organization and where he is going, but a vision is of little value unless it is shared in a way so as to generate enthusiasm and commitment."
—Claude Taylor

Inspiration

"He taught us to care because he cared. He taught us to be concerned because he was concerned. He taught us that honesty is sacred, is absolute and is eternal."
—Frank Broyles

"For when that One Great Scorer comes to mark against your name, He writes not that you won or lost, but how you played the game."
—Grantland Rice

"Be the change you want to see."
—Gandhi

Motivation

"Motivation is a fire from within. If someone else tries to light that fire under you, chances are it will burn very briefly."
—Stephen Covey

"Motivating people—the ingredient that separates winners from losers."
—Bear Bryant

"Motivate by letting players know the one who puts out the most effort will finish the game on the floor."

—Unknown

Potential

"If we did the things we are capable of, we would astound ourselves."

—Thomas Edison

"Every game is a chance to measure yourself against your own potential."

—Bud Wilkerson

"You will become as small as your controlling desire, as great as your dominant aspiration."

—James Allen

"Some men are bigger, faster, stronger, and smarter than others—but not a single man has a corner on dreams, desire, or ambition."

—Duffy Daugherty

"Big decisions wouldn't be big if they didn't have life-changing implications."

—Jim Moore

Goals

"Goals achieved with little effort are seldom appreciated and give no personal satisfaction."

—Bob Devaney

Mental Toughness

"If I can beat a guy in his mind, everything else falls into place."

—Dan Dierdorf

"I want to coach a team that opponents don't look forward to playing."

—Danny Ford

"Mental toughness is many things. It is humility because it behooves all of us to remember that simplicity is the sign of greatness and meekness is the sign of true strength. Mental toughness is Spartanism with qualities of sacrifice, self-denial, dedication. It is fearlessness, and it is love."

—Vince Lombardi

"Everyone will get beat sometime physically, but a
champion seldom gets beat mentally."
—Chuck Knoll

Appealing to Pride

"Oh, excuse me, ladies! I thought this was the Notre Dame locker room."
— Knute Rockne, poking his head
inside the door of the locker room after
his team had been mauled in the first
half of a game

"If you're gonna be a winner, you got to have a bad case of the wants."
—Erik Russell

Teamwork/Team Concept

"I play not my eleven best but my best eleven that think as one."
—Knute Rockne

"In order to have a winner, the team must have a feeling of unity. Every player must
put the team first, ahead of personal glory. Morale is the key to winning."
—Bear Bryant

"We may have come in different ships, but we're all in the same boat now."
—Charlie McClendon

"Our goal is not to win. It's to play together and play hard.
Then, winning takes care of itself."
—Mike Krzyzewski

"Every time you put on a team jersey, make sure you play for the
name on the front of the jersey, not the one on the back."
—Unknown

"They say you win with your five best players, but I found you
win with the five who fit together best."
—Red Auerbach

"The challenge of every team is to build a feeling of oneness, of dependence
on one another because the question is usually not how well
each person performs, but how well they work together."
—Vince Lombardi

"One finger can't lift a pebble."
—Hopi tribal saying

"Never treat your second team like second class"
—Jim Moore

Victories Off the Field

"If we win the national championship, so what? It sounds cornball, but that's the way I feel. My best team will be one that produces the best doctors, lawyers, fathers, and citizens, not necessarily the one with the best record. Let's keep football in context."
—Joe Paterno

"Everyone is a role model to someone and your impact might not be know for 25 or 30 years."
—Tom Osborne

Trust, Respect, Coaching

"If you respect a player and he respects you, then you have a relationship, and in a relationship all commentary is allowed."
—Bill Parcells

"The coach is the team, and the team is the coach. You reflect each other."
—Tommy Prothro

"Either love your players or get out of coaching."
—Bobby Dodd

"Never leave the field with a boy feeling you're mad at him. You can chew him out on the field, but then pat him on the shoulder in the locker room."
—Jake Gaither

"You have to learn what makes Sammy run. For one player, it is a pat on the back. For another, it's chewing him or her out. For still another, it's a fatherly talk. You are a fool if you think, as I did as a young coach, that you can treat them all alike."
—Bear Bryant

"Coaching is about human interaction and trying to know your players."
—Bill Parcells

"Coach a boy as if he were you own son."
—Eddie Robinson

Assistant Coaches

"No head coach can be better than his staff. Show me a winning team,
and I'll show you a good group of assistant coaches."
—Johnny Majors

Scrutiny

"A coach isn't as smart as they say he is when he wins, or as stupid when he loses."
—Darrell Royal

"If you're a football coach, criticism comes with the territory. If it tears
you up, you better get into another profession."
—Pat Dye

"To err is human, to forgive is divine. But to forgive a ball coach is unheard of."
—Vince Dooley

Other

"You control your life by controlling your time."
—Hyrum W. Smith

"It's what you learn after you know it all that counts."
—John Wooden

"Know what you want and believe that you can have it."
—Norman Vincent Peale

"The things we have to learn before we can do them, we learn by doing them."
—Aristotle

"It is amazing what you can accomplish if you do not care who gets the credit."
—William James

"He who refuses to embrace a unique opportunity loses the
prize as surely as if he tried and failed."
—William James

"The harder you work, the harder it is to surrender."
—Vince Lombardi

"Dumb players do dumb things. Smart players seldom do dumb things."
—Bill Parcells

"There has got to be a special place in heaven for coaches' wives."
—Bear Bryant

"Every time a player goes out there, at least 20 people have some influence on him. His momma has more influence than anyone."
—Bear Bryant

"Don't talk too much or too soon."
—Bear Bryant

"I cannot give you a formula for success, but I can give you the formula for failure: try to please everybody."
—Bob Devaney

"I never watched an athlete become a champion that I didn't smell sweat."
—Alonzo Smith "Jake" Gaither

"Failures are expected by losers, ignored by winners."
—Joe Gibbs

"Great truth is simple, so also are great coaches."
—John Heisman

"The difference between a successful person and others is not a lack of knowledge, but rather in a lack of will."
—Vince Lombardi

"Work hard, keep your mouth shut, and good things will happen."
—George Perles

"You can only coast one way, whether it be in sports or business, and that's downhill."
—Knute Rockne

"If you have men who will come only if they know there is a good road, I don't want them. I want men who will come if there is no road at all."

—Dr. Livingston, during a mission to Africa, in response to another missionary organization who wanted to send assistance to him and wrote, "Have you found any good roads to where you are? If so, we want to send other men to join you."

Top Ten Tips for Public Speaking

If you are not used to speaking to crowds in a public arena, the following are a few basic tips that might help you. In coaches' speak, these tips are the fundamentals. Before the speech, breathe deep to relax, smile (actually practice smiling), and know you have something good you are about to share with your audience. Most importantly, have fun with your speech. People want you to do well.

- Be prepared. You wouldn't go into a game without a game plan. Do not go into a speech without one, either. Know who your audience is and have a good idea what they are looking for. Funny, inspirational, informational, etc. Keep in mind that people generally are most nervous when they are the least prepared. If you are prepared and have something to say, you have no reason to be nervous.

- Have a plan. Bring notes, but don't read them to the crowd. Talk to the crowd using your notes. Write headlines only, such as, "Our team looks great this year," and then simply speak from your heart.

- Know how long you are supposed to speak. There is nothing worse than addressing a crowd and having them start to walk out because you are taking too long. People will be very attentive if you tell them how long you "have been asked to speak."

- Always thank them for coming or for having you. If you want them to appreciate you, you must first show that you appreciate them.

- Make eye contact. Make as much eye contact as possible and slow down your pace of speech. Most people talk way too fast! Let people comprehend what you are saying.

- Don't fumble with keys or change in your pocket. And, have someone else adjust and test the microphone. Let the problems happen with them.

- Be respectful of the audience. Rooms can be filled with uninformed people who ask ridiculous questions. Respect them anyway and realize others are wondering the same thing. Thank people for their questions.

- If you cough or sneeze, say, "Excuse me," and move on. It is not that big of a deal.

- Be mindful of what you say about players. Don't just talk about the superstars. Parents of less talented players will be hanging on your every word.

- Be positive. People want to hear an encouraging word even in difficult situations. Remember: these folks want to support your program. They want to hear from you. They will be listening.

Speeches You Can Use

It seems all coaches at some point have to deliver a speech. Following are several useful ideas for different situations.

Team Speach for Coaches: "I Knew We Became a Team When ..."
(The following speech can be delivered to coaches at a coaches' clinic.)

It's good to be here with you today, and it probably won't surprise you to learn that I am here to remind you of something you already know: "*Teamwork* is more fun and more productive."

Many of you have forgotten more about football than I will ever know, but I do know this: if you get your players to believe in one another and see a clear, obtainable goal, then there is nothing you cannot achieve. I also have to confess this will not be a speech. This will be an interactive session on how to make this group of players a true team.

I once heard of a coach who would continually say to his players, "I knew we became a team when ..." He would say things like, "I knew we became a team when our kicker missed a very important field goal and the other players surrounded him on the sideline supporting him. I knew we became a team when we lost the first two games of the season but no one gave up and we came back to win a championship." You have to ask yourselves, "When did my group become a team?"

I want you to turn to a coach next to you and tell him, "I knew we became a team when ..." and finish the statement from the team you coach now or one you coached in the past. If you are having a hard time finishing this, then you will really enjoy and benefit from the rest of our time.

(Take a few minutes.)

Okay, let's share a few minutes. Please say your name and where you coach. How did you finish the phrase, "I knew we became a team when ..." ? Please stand up and share so we can learn from your experience.

Excellent! Now, that's what I am talking about. Now, there are several keys to becoming a team. Coach Wooden always said, "Give me five players who work as a team and we will beat anyone." From what you said, you know how great it is when your players "get it" and begin acting as one. The problem is this: How do you get there? What does it take to get to that level? Let's be specific:

One of the first things you must do to become a team is to begin to rely on one another and trust each other. To rely on one another. All of you have to figure things out all day long. Who's going to play this week? What play should I call? The list goes on and on. And you are very good at this. You are smart and you know the smartest coaches and players can think on their feet. Do you agree?

Let's take a quiz to see how well you do. It's a Mensa quiz (see Figures 9-1 and 9-2), and I have given it hundreds of times. Try to figure out on your own how many answers you can get in three minutes. For example: 7 doaw = seven days of a week. (Allow coaches to take the test.)

Okay, how did you do? I see a lot of ink. You look like you were taking the SAT or something. I could see the smoke rising. Now, let's do it in groups of four. You have the same three minutes. (Allow coaches to take the test again, working together.)

How did you do? Why did I have you do that? Because as I said earlier, it's more fun and more productive to work together. You guys sit in your office and agonize over what to do with a particular player. Your player in the midst of a game looks across the line and in his head says, "I can't cover this guy. He is way too fast." The truth is: individually, we can't; together we can! When you pool your talents and your knowledge, it is incredible what you can do.

Who did you play high school football for? Think back. Did you learn something there? Of course, you did. Who played college football? Did you learn things you can share? Of course, the bottom line is: when you work together it is incredible what you can do.

Parents' Meetings

Parents who attend parents' meetings arrive for a variety of reasons. Some may want to see for themselves if what they have been hearing about you is true. Other parents will only be there because their son or daughter told them they had to be there. Still others will be there simply to find out the details of the upcoming season, such as when and where practices will be held and where they can get a game schedule.

However, all of them have come because they want to hear what you have to say and how you and your program will benefit their child (see Chapter 5). Be careful not to talk about specific players. The only parents interested in your star player are that player's parents. The other parents want to hear about the team and the program. This meeting is a golden opportunity for you to lay a foundation with parents that you desperately need them as a part of your team.

Parent's Pre-Season Speech: "It Truly Takes a Village, On and Off the Field"

Thank you for coming tonight. I know you are all anxious about the upcoming season, as am I. I am Coach _____ and I have been given the *privilege* of coaching your son or daughter this year. As the saying goes, "It takes a village to raise a child." Believe me, I realize it does.

Team Mensa Quiz

Instructions: Work out what the letters mean in each phrase. According to MENSA, if you get 19 or more correct, you are a "genius." Only two MENSA members achieved full marks. See how well you do.

Scoring: 1 to 5 = Average, 6 to 11 = Somewhat Intelligent, 12 to 18 = Intelligent, 19 or more = Genius

No.	Cryptic
0	24 H in a D
1	26 L of the A
2	7 D of the W
3	7 W of the W
4	12 S of the Z
5	66 B of the B
6	52 C in a P (WJs)
7	13 S in the USF
8	18 H on a G C
9	39 B of the O T
10	5 T on a F
11	90 D in a R A
12	3 B M (S H T R)
13	32 is the T in D F at which W F
14	4 q in a D
15	3 W on a T
16	55 mph
17	11 P in a F (S) T
18	12 M in a Y
19	4 Q l a G
20	8 T on a O
21	29 D in F in a L Y
22	27 B in the N T
23	365 D in a Y
24	13 L in a B D
25	52 W in a Y
26	9 L of a C
27	60 M in a H
28	16 O in a pd.
29	64 S on a C B
30	100 yds in a FF
31	3 o b i
32	1000 Y in a M
33	25 c l a Q

Figure 9-1. Team Mensa Quiz

Team Mensa Quiz Answer Key

No.	Cryptic
0	24 hours in a day
1	26 letters of the alphabet
2	7 days of the week
3	7 wonders of the world
4	12 signs of the zodiac
5	66 books of the Bible
6	52 cards in a pack (without jokers)
7	13 stripes in the United States Flag
8	18 holes on a golf course
9	39 books of the Old Testament
10	5 toes on a foot
11	90 degrees in a Right Angle
12	3 blind mice (see how they run)
13	32 is the temperature in degrees Fahrenheit
14	4 quarters in a dollar
15	3 wheels on a tricycle
16	55 miles per hour
17	11 players in a football or soccer team
18	12 months in a year
19	4 quarts in a gallon
20	8 tentacles on a octopus
21	29 days in February in a leap year
22	27 books in the New Testament
23	365 days in a year
24	13 loaves in a baker's dozen
25	52 weeks in a year
26	9 lives of a cat
27	60 minutes in an hour
28	16 ounces in a pound
29	64 squares on a checker board (chess)
30	100 yards in a football field
31	3 outs per inning
32	1000 years in a millennium
33	25 cents in a quarter

Figure 9-2. Team Mensa Quiz Answer Key

I want you to know that it really *is* a privilege for me to coach your child. Not everyone in this world gets to do what he loves to do and still make a living. I do. I also want you to know that I understand that with privilege also comes responsibility.

In the next few months, I will be spending a lot of time with your son/daughter. I desperately want everybody on this team to become a better ballplayer, and our staff will do all they can to make sure that happens. But even more than that, we want them to become better people, and we will also do all we can to make sure that happens.

Coaches are in the business of molding young, impressionable players, and we realize that. We realize these are young men and women, and we know that their lives consist of more than just sports. But anyone who has ever played a team sport will attest that being a part of the team was a great time. I think that playing ball makes for a better memory than experience because we will work these players harder than they have ever worked before.

I wanted you, as parents, to be here tonight because as much time as I spend with them and as much as I teach them and as hard as I work them, I also realize that I will never have the influence on them that you have. Bear Bryant, a college football coach, once said, "Every time a player goes out there, at least 20 people have some amount of influence on him. His mother has more influence than anyone. I know because I played, and I loved my mama." Bear Bryant understood the importance of a player's family and the importance of having the support of that family. I also understand that what happens at home will play a big part in how successful our team will be this year. And I want us to be successful.

I am asking you to help our team by encouraging your son or daughter. To help our team by monitoring your son or daughter, to make sure they are eating right and keeping up with their schoolwork. I am asking you to lift them up when they are down and to ask them to take out the trash when they are too "up." And remind them, "Never let anyone outwork you." In essence, I am asking you—each one of you—to be a part of this team. That is how you, as a parent, can contribute to the success of our season. We need your help and want your help, but where I need your help is at home. Please let us coach. Our pledge is that we will be fair to your son or daughter.

[You will now have the parents' attention. Now is a good time to talk about your policy for playing time. For example: playing time is earned, players missing practice will not play, everyone plays, etc. As the season goes on, that will become your biggest "sticky" issue. Refer to Chapter 5.]

As with every team, we will have players whose skills and abilities will be superior to other players. However, kids who hustle and work hard always give themselves a chance to play. This is a team. It takes all of us. Only so many players can be on the field/court at a time. But it will take all of these boys and girls to achieve success.

Our goal is to make every player better—as an athlete and as a person. Those who are starting every week, we will work with them and push them and coach them to improve. We have the same commitment to the players who are not seeing as much playing time. We will work hard to help them improve. We will work with all the players in hopes of helping them become better athletes.

Baylor's women's basketball coach Kim Mulkey-Robertson said, "She [referring to Sophia Young] makes me look good. She has lived up to the hype and scored 33 points and added 12 rebounds on her way to being the all-time Big-12 scoring champion." All any coach can ask is to teach players and let them use their God-given ability to excel. When asked about the scoring-title possibility, Sophia Young responded, "I didn't even know about any records until you guys [the media] brought it up." Some athletes have their priorities in order and, of course, coaches help them get things straight.

We realize that success for a coach is not necessarily wins on the field but wins off the field. If your son or daughter improves this year, then we have been successful.

One more thing: we believe in praise and encouragement, but we also believe in accountability, hard work, and loyalty. There will be times this season when you may not like me very much—and that's okay. All I ask is that you be careful what you say in front of your son.

You are entrusting me with your son. If you want to speak to me about anything, I am available. I am available Monday through Friday from _____[Provide the times. You will need to be specific.]. I am not available to discuss anything except an emergency on the day of a game. Please do not approach me after the game about our booster club fundraiser or about your son or daughter's position on the team. Emotions are high after a game—win or lose. It is not a good time. I promise, I will not approach you at your office after you have either just lost or closed a big deal.

I also am not available immediately before or after practice. If you need to contact me, please do so during my conference hour. I definitely have an open-door policy, as do all of my coaches.

[Discuss practice and game schedules, as well as a typical game day timeline. Then, introduce your assistant coaches, their spouses, and your spouse, if applicable.]

We want victories on the field/court, but we also want them off the field/court—and we are committed to your athlete. If you will allow me one more Bear Bryant quote, I will finish and take questions. Bear Bryant said, "When we have a good team, I know it's because we have boys that come from good mommas and papas."

Coach's Speech at Banquet

First of all, I want to thank you for being here and for celebrating with your team.

Certainly this year has been a successful season for all of us. Even though I do not always stress wins and losses as the definition of being a winning team, every one of you has played like a champion. To me, a champion is someone in life who displays character at all times—even when no one is looking. A champion gives his or her all at all times. Our players and coaches have all done that.

It is a privilege to get to coach such fine young people. The truth is I would be honored to call any of these young people my son or daughter. I am deeply aware of the sacrifices that many of you have made this past year to get us where we are. Without your hard work and loyalty, we would not have made it nor be able to go where we are headed.

I do know one thing. It has not always been easy this season, and yet our goal is clear: to offer the best in athletics and, more importantly, the opportunity for every player to grow as outstanding citizens. We're on the right track in obtaining our goal. This year, we've actually reached our goals by: [Provide at least three detailed ways in which the team has achieved its goals.] I believe, whole-heartedly, that many other accolades and awards will follow, and you will make it happen with individual effort and teamwork—one person at a time.

I know I always preach this and I always will: Your loyalty is clear and I must admit, I am overwhelmed by it. At the same time, I feel honored and humbled to be entrusted to coach this team. Yet I am only one piece of this big team picture. Now is the time for all of us to focus and work with a renewed passion. We will work together, side by side, to achieve our long-range goal. We will reach this goal together and we will all reap the benefits. Nothing compares to being part of a winning team that you help build.

As you already know, every challenge this team has faced together has propelled us to reach our next goal. However—and you know this, too—it has taken every person doing his part to make it happen. Our tradition called upon each of you to personally challenge and commit yourself. As we said at the onset of the season, we will provide the training; you provide the passion. And you did!

Let's face it: an amount of pride is associated with a winner. A great deal of satisfaction and security results when you know you are closely aligned with an organization that has set the delivery bar high and has accomplished its goals. Success always requires diligence, determination, perseverance, and passion. These qualities are very powerful forces. These are the forces that will continue to carry you to your destination.

Again, thank you, and have a good time tonight celebrating. You deserve the fun. Go _____!

Motivational Speech: "What Is Your I.M.P.A.C.T.?"
[The following speech can be used for parents, boosters, and/or other coaches.]

What is your impact? Do you know? Before I continue, I want to tell you about [start by telling a joke, possibly the Little Train Conductor from the next section].

I know you all take your jobs very seriously. It shows in many ways. [Give examples, especially if some people have done some significant things.] Now, I want to mention something. Let's learn what your I.M.P.A.C.T. really is. What kind of impact do you really make?

It's incredible what you can do for students changing their lives. We always talk about the impact that we make as an organization. For a minute, I would like to discuss the impact you make. If you break down the word "impact," the acronym points out some key messages and questions for us all. [Use dry-erase board/chalkboard/PowerPoint to write out and explain.]

- I stands for image. What do you project? Crucial for yourself and your players.
- M stands for motivation. What is your motivation? People are usually motivated by one of four things: money, social reasons, the challenge of the job and pride that they know they have a job that is important and they are excited to perform it, knowing they help others. What motivates you? It is important to know.
- P stands for the concept of preparation. Are you ready for different situations?
- A stands for action. Move, act, show energy. You have a mission. Barbara Jordan showed action in all she did. She broke all kinds of barriers throughout her life. If she were an athlete, she would have been a world-class hurdler because she spent her whole life leaping over barriers with grace and dexterity. She broke records.
- C helps you learn subtle ways to show confidence. You are the expert, and they are looking to you.
- T stands for trusting. Be a trustworthy person that people can count on with integrity. The big key to trusting each other is to be able to rely on one another. Take what you do seriously and think about the impact you make.

Thanks for coming, thanks for listening, and thank you for your impact on this team.

Inspiration, Not Motivation

I want to begin with a little quiz:

- Who are the three richest people in the world?
- Who is the CEO of the biggest company in the United States?

- Who won the Pulitzer Prize or Nobel Prize this year?
- Who won the Heisman Trophy last year?
- Who won the Oscar for the Best Actor?
- Who won Miss America?

Do the names of these famous people escape you, even as famous as they are? The truth is: fame is fleeting, and even though these people are tops in their field and probably wealthy beyond imagination, they still don't begin to be as important or memorable as so many others. Though the world and media seem to portray them as world leaders and famous, the truth is we can't even remember their names.

Another short quiz:

- Who was your first-grade teacher who taught you to count?
- What principal saw something in you that you never saw yourself?
- What coach helped bring out gifts you never knew you had?
- And who are the people you want to spend your time with and whom you enjoy?

The truth is: the most important people in the world are not the ones with incredible credentials or the most money. The most important people in the world are the ones you remember and who care about you, true?

I know many of you, and I know you care about those you have been trusted to teach, coach, or lead. And you will be remembered. Those of you who have been around this profession can attest to this. How many times have you been out in public and had someone come up to you from years past and say, "Hey, you were my fifth-grade teacher and you were the best!" You may not have remembered their names, but they sure remembered yours.

We are fortunate to be in a field where we truly make a difference. Do you realize how many people go to work every day and who would love the opportunity to help people and to be able to truly change lives? Many people think what we do is to motivate others or to encourage kids, and that is true. But what I really think we do is to inspire them to motivate themselves.

Do you see the difference? If we motivate them, that's great but it doesn't last when we leave. When you truly inspire kids, you help them see what strengths they have inside themselves—those strengths that will last a lifetime and help them through situations we can't even begin to imagine. You have an opportunity to teach them life lessons. Lessons involving basic things like respect, dignity, and the importance of keeping commitments.

And, you take your job seriously, I know, but surely it's not for the money? No, you do it because of the satisfaction you get from giving of yourself and because others did it for you. We do take our jobs seriously. The only problem is, we can't keep doing things the same old way.

You know as well as I do, the kids we deal with these days live in a different world than the world in which we grew up—and that's not all bad:

- Kids today wouldn't dream of moving in a car without wearing a seatbelt.
- If they can afford it, parents wouldn't dare let their kids leave their house today without a cell phone to keep track of them. We wandered wherever we wanted and played in creeks and who knows what else.
- They don't have to take a vacation without a DVD player. We slept on the back of the car on our trips where the speakers are now.
- We had station wagons, not mini-vans or SUVs.
- We ate Mom's good ol' fried chicken—certainly not chicken nuggets.

Most of us lived with our parents in the same house and had adults around us who also guided us. Many of the kids today are starving for leadership and looking for those good voices. The problem today is that modern conveniences are hindering kids and their development. In our day, if you wanted to talk to your friends, what did you do? Of course, you either walked or rode your bike to their house. You got a little exercise.

Playing baseball or football meant grabbing a ball and heading to a nearby field with our friends. Now, it means picking up a Game Boy.

In our day, at least kids would go outside and play when they had to wait for their favorite TV show. Now, they can watch whatever they want whenever they want because of on-demand cable or DVDs—and don't even get me started on the Internet. Kids are different these days and have different demands. Youth obesity and apathy is at an all-time high and we must respond.

This fall, we will be instituting some new programs to try and help our kids escape this newest epidemic. It would be irresponsible for us not to. [You may tell them about some of the new exciting things here, but keep it short. Not too many details, just the program and what the students will gain from the programs.]

The old adage is true: do the same old things and get the same old results. I will not be satisfied with status quo, and I know you won't be, either. There will be those who will complain. There will also be those who will give us all kinds of reasons why we can't make those changes. There is only one voice we need to listen to and that is the voice of that child—big or small—who will say, in many ways and not only with their voices, "I need your help." We must respond, just as someone once did for us.

We need to remember those who once led us, those who encouraged us to go into this profession by their example. It is true. They never had to deal with issues like school finances or the tests we have to deal with today, but they had their own issues, issues we never knew about. We must change as the world is changing around us and become proactive.

We have good news on several fronts. First, today we understand children and their needs better than ever before. When we see the kids we are trying to inspire, we need to remember new information is available. Even though all these kids are different, they do have one thing in common and that is the need to have leaders around them who care and who lead by example.

We have known for years you can't talk to every kid the same way. They all are wired differently and respond to different things. Even though this is a new way at looking at those we serve, it might explain why certain kids do what they do. We can't judge what we don't understand, and if this breakdown of kids into different personality types helps us better understand one child, it is worth considering. Of course, the best way to understand kids is to look into their eyes, see through to their hearts, and let them know we are there for them.

One more point to consider is that all too often we don't hear "Thank you," and maybe don't get as many pats on the backs as we deserve. I am here today to say, "You are appreciated and may never know the incredible influence you have."

However, the following quote from Indira Gandhi is a good reminder that getting credit isn't everything: "My grandfather once told me that there were two kinds of people: those who do the work and those who take the credit. He told me to try to be in the first group; there was much less competition." Remember also the proverb that says: "Where there is no vision, the people perish." Kids are starving for our attention and need our leadership desperately.

The other bit of good news is that we serve on a team as we work with others. We have all heard the sayings about teamwork, and they are all true. John Wooden said, "Don't give me a star. Give me five good players who play as a team and we will win more often than not." Did he know what he was talking about? Well, he won 11 out of 13 national championships in basketball.

We all bring different gifts and talents to the table and our combined experiences make us an incredible force. You _____[pick someone you know] worked at _____ school district before you came here and can now share knowledge you learned there. You _____ earned _____ degree and can know share what you know with the rest of us. As individuals, we are pretty good, but as a team we are unbeatable. Together, we really can make an impact and never feel alone.

Halftime and Pre-Game Speeches

Halftime and pre-game speeches are thought to be excellent motivators for teams. Nothing is better to motivate a team than hard work and preparation. The pre-game speech should be more a reminder of what teams have planned and practiced for. It is amazing what happens in locker rooms when coaches are excited and players are nervous.

Keys to a Great Pre-Game Speech*

"You have to make them believe in you. If they don't believe in you,
it's a problem. That makes it difficult to win ball games."
—Roy Simmons, Jr.

"I always try to take the focus off what the other team is doing and put it back more that it's about us and you want to prove that you're the best at what you do game in and game out. If you can get them to believe in that philosophy, you'll get them further in the game. I try to get players focused on the little things and how important they are to the end result rather than just focusing on the end result. It's not all about beating the other team; it's about you and how you play. That's something a kid can build on forever."
—Gary Gait

"The key things to me are that it's more of an opportunity to review the game plan and the specific personnel and what you're trying to accomplish. You have to make sure the team is very clear on that and usually most of it can be taken care of during warm-ups. The pre-game speech is not a time to learn new information. There should be no new info—maybe some small bits, opposing players who are scratched from the lineup—but you can't information-dump on them because there's no way they can put anything new in their heads. You should be like a pilot before takeoff, going through a little checklist of things."
—Dave Huntley

"The pre-game speeches where I'm most open with my players about my feelings and my path is where they've really responded the best. When I'm letting them know how much I care about them, that strikes a chord inside them. The coach striking those chords really makes a difference."
—Tom Ryan

"I think a young kid probably feels enough pressure anyway to perform as an individual and a teammate so to push that pressure to a higher level in a pre-game speech, you're probably not going to get a better performance. Trying to break the natural tension with a little chuckle, I think, is real important."
—Roy Simmons III

*The quotations in this section are from Inside Lacrosse (www.insidelacrosse.com).

"If you're playing a weak sister, sometimes you have to point to other situations where there have been upsets. In sports, nothing is a given. You have to earn it every day. You have to point to some of the things you need to do to be successful that day. What happens in games like that is people get point-hungry. You have to stay with the game plan. That has to be paramount. That's what good teams do: stay with the game plan regardless of the opponent."

—Les Bartley

"I think the key for young coaches is to not get frustrated. What you see in your head and what the players see in their heads are probably two different things. It takes a long time to communicate that. Players will nod their heads and totally not understand. You have to stay positive no matter what. If you lose, go down trying your butt off. Don't start sniping. It adds to the agony of the season."

—Darris Kilgour

"A game is not determined by the pre-game speech, but the first several minutes can be. It gives you a chance to seize momentum emotionally if you're in the right frame of mind and something good happens. If you get that first goal, it can give you an advantage."

—Richie Meade

"You gotta keep things in perspective. It's a game; it's meant to be a release. It's not a life-or-death situation. It's something kids derive some enjoyment from and you need to approach it that way. I watch some of these team camps during the summer and some of these guys are a little over the edge. At some point you need to relax and just enjoy playing the game."

—Dave Urick

"If I don't have some personal motivation going into the game, what is said isn't going to motivate me. But what a good speech can do is really crystallize my focus, really make it laser-sharp when I'm on the floor. I think that's pretty powerful. When it comes to our level of the sport where everybody is so close, having that razor-sharp focus going out, especially in one-goal games, makes so much of a difference."

—Pat Coyle

Speech for When Things Are Not Going Well at Halftime, or Pre-Game Before Facing an Overmatched Opponent

[Coaches and teams want to win. However, having heart and being willing to fight are often what separates winners from losers, as the following story demonstrates.]

The Alamo walls were crumbling. The soldiers were tired and weary. They had been fighting for 12 days. The odds were certainly against them. The enemy soldiers appeared to be superior. The enemy felt as those they had them right where they wanted them. It didn't look good for the Texas soldiers. The Texas soldiers had two options fight on or surrender, quit, give up.

Those options were the only two they had—fight or give up. Those were their only options. Those are the only options we have right now: we can fight on, or we can surrender.

According to legend, Colonel William B. Travis pulled out his sword and drew a line on the ground inside the Alamo. He asked anyone who was willing to stay and fight to step over the line. The tired and wounded and overmatched soldiers one by one crossed over the line. One soldier who was wounded asked his friends to carry him across the line because even though he was wounded, he wanted to fight on.

It is about bravery and courage and willing to fight for what we believe in. Do you have that courage? Are you willing to fight?

[Use the threshold of the locker room door or draw a line on the ground.]

This doorway, this line to the field/court is our line on the Alamo floor. I am asking anyone who is willing to fight on to cross over. You may be beat down, you may be uncertain, but all I am asking of you is to fight (or fight on). Today, let those who watch you play be moved by your courage and your willingness to fight to the end.

[Although they lost the battle of the Alamo, their willingness to fight delayed Santa Anna's advance. They also inspired others to fight the Mexican Army and eventually win independence for Texas.]

Quick Stories for Pep Rallies

It Is Not How You Start, but How You Finish

It was opening day in 1954, and the Cincinnati Reds were playing the then-Milwaukee Braves in a baseball game. It was the much-anticipated debut for two young ball players, one a rookie for the Braves and one a center fielder for the Reds. The center fielder for the Reds was a young man by the name of Jim Greengrass. He had a strong arm and a quick bat. That day, Jim Greengrass went 4-for-4, hitting four doubles to set an opening-day record for doubles in one game. The rookie for the Braves that day didn't fair quite as well. As a matter of fact he went 0-for-5 – striking out four times. His name was: Henry "Hank" Aaron. Hank Aaron, of course, went on to become a great player and currently holds the Major League record for homeruns with 755. In 1982, he was enshrined into the Baseball Hall of Fame. If you have never heard of Jim Greengrass, you are not alone. After his fabulous opening day, he was hardly ever heard from again. The moral of the story is simple: it is not how you start that matters most; it is how you finish.

> "Trying to throw a fastball by Hank Aaron was like trying to sneak a sunrise past a rooster."
>
> —Curt Simmons, former Major League pitcher

Attitude: What Are You Looking for Today?

What is your attitude today? Are you looking for the best in people, or are you looking for the worst? Are you glad you are here, or do you resent it? Think of two birds: the buzzard and the hummingbird. What does the buzzard look for each day? The answer: the buzzard looks for dead things. Buzzards will circle and circle in the air until they finally find something dead.

What does the hummingbird look for each day? The answer: the hummingbird looks for flowers and nectar. The hummingbird will buzz and buzz in the air until it finds what it is looking for. The buzzard finds things that are dead because that is what it is looking for each day. The hummingbird finds nectar because that is what it is looking for each day. When it comes to attitude, we usually find what we are looking for each day.

If we come looking for something to complain about, we will surely find it. If we come looking for ways to do an outstanding job and to be a better team player, chances are we will find exactly what we are looking for today. Your outlook and attitude are your choice.

Leaders Will Lead

Mahatma Gandhi was an agent of change. Gandhi did not only call a nation and world to change, he modeled change. He did not only call others to sacrifice. He, himself, sacrificed. Gandhi once said, "Be the change you want to see." If you are a leader of people, then you have a vision for the people you lead. Undoubtedly, you want your team to be a productive and cohesive team serving a common goal.

Do you want to see your team more passionate about their goals? How do they deal with the challenges? What kind of rapport do they have with each other? Do they buy into and live the company motto and mission? Are they punctual and respectful? Are they passionate about their goals? Are you?

Leaders will lead and followers will follow. If you lead down the path of monotony and tedium, a few will follow. If you lead down the path of passion and commitment, more will follow. You are the leader, so lead by example. Be the change you want to see.

Want Things to Be Different? Are You Insane?

Following is a simple "if, then" axiom to remember when dealing with people: If you want things to be different, then you must do things differently. Albert Einstein is quoted as having said that the definition of insanity is, "Doing the same thing over and over again and expecting a different result." Insanity is wishing your team would win more games but not equipping them with the tools or the inspiration to do so. Insanity is hoping things will get better without attending games or cheering the team. One thing's for sure. You can't wish yourself out of a rut. If you continue to spin your wheels, only half-heartedly supporting your team, then you only dig yourself into a deeper rut.

Today, we want your commitment to get behind the _____. To cheer them on, to show your support, and to let them know you're behind this team, 100 percent. If you want things to be different, then you must do things differently.

Coaching Stories and Jokes

"People often say that motivation doesn't last. Well, neither does bathing—that's why we recommend if daily."

—Zig Ziglar.

The Coach Who Stuttered

A coach got fired one day because his boosters and athletic director said he was a poor communicator, so he went out looking for a job. As he was walking down the street, he saw a sign in a window that read: "Encyclopedia Salesman Wanted."

The coach decided that sounded like a pretty good deal, being an educator and all, so he went inside. He told the manager he could sell encyclopedias. The manager looked him over and asked, "Have you ever sold anything before?"

"Well, n-n-no, b-b-but I can, can sell," he said, with a terrible speech impediment.

"Well, okay," the manager said, kind of hesitating because of the man's stuttering. "Why don't you give it a try. They are $200 per set."

The coach left very excited and in about 30 minutes, he showed back up with $200 and said, "Okay, okay boooss. Give me, two two moooore sets."

The boss said, "Well, all right." And one hour later the coach showed back up with $400. The manager was happy and somewhat amazed. "If you don't mind my asking, how in the world can you sell so many encyclopedias?"

"Well," said the crafty ol' coach. "I, I, I, just go up to to to someone oneees hous, house and say say, 'Ah Ma'am, you uuu wannnt tooo tooo buy a seeet offff ennclloopeddiassss orrrr dooooo yoooouu just want meeee mmeeee toooo stand here and read theee whooole thing tooo you?"

Ferocious

Earl Campbell, the Heisman-winning running back, said he was only the second-best football player in his family. On several occasions, he said his older brother Fred was a much better player. His brother played linebacker for John Tyler High School and while he was very tough, he may not have been real smart. One night during a game in which John Tyler was not playing very well, his coach called time-out and called Fred over to the sideline. With all the forcefulness he could muster, the coach said, "Fred, I want you to go back out there and I want you to get ferocious! Get ferocious right now!"

"Okay," said Fred, and he turned around and ran back on the field. Then he stopped, stood for a few minutes and looked at the other players on defense, one by one. Finally he called time-out and returned to the sideline. "Uh, coach? Uh, which one of them is Ferocious?"

I Run Things

After being eloquently introduced, a coach stood at the podium and stared at the crowd. Finally, with a serious face, he began speaking, slowly and deliberately. "It's true. I run this football team. At home, I run things as well." Everyone gasped. "That's right. At home when I am not coaching, I run the vacuum cleaner, I run the dishwasher, the lawnmower, or whatever else my wife wants me to do."

The Little Train Conductor

A little boy who was a train conductor took his job very seriously. One day, sitting in front of his train set, the little boy put on his conductor hat and said in a rather stern voice, "Okay, all you sorry little people that want to get on the train, get on the train. All you sorry people that want to get off the train, get off."

Well, his mother heard him, came in and said, "Johnny, we don't talk that way in our house. Now, I want you to go into your room and stay in there 15 minutes before you come back out."

"Okay," he said, and he took his train conductor hat off and went into his room and stayed exactly 15 minutes. He then came out, put his hat back on and said (in a really nice, slow tone), "Okay, all you nice little people that want to get on board, come aboard. All you nice little people that want to get off the train, you may get off. (Changing his tough tone back a bit) And all you people hacked off about the 15-minute delay, see the witch in the kitchen."

Don't Listen to Everyone

These negative voices remind me of the old man and the little boy who were walking their donkey through their small town. People on the sidewalks saw the two walking the animal and said, "Look, those two are walking the donkey. They should let the old man ride on the donkey's back." So, they did.

As they walked a little farther, someone else complained and said, "Look at that man riding the donkey. The child should be riding." So, they lifted the little boy on board as well. A little farther down the road, people complained because both the boy and old man were riding the donkey. Finally the boy and man heard the complaints and decided to not ride the donkey but to carry the big animal, especially over a bridge that was coming. The problem was, they accidentally dropped the donkey in the water as they went over the bridge. Whoosh!

The moral of the story: if you listen to all your critiques, you will lose your…donkey.

Paint the Porch

Players today are so smart and so sophisticated. A while back, though, they weren't nearly as smart and just did what they were told. A coach's wife told her husband to paint the porch on their house one day. As a matter of fact, she told him on several occasions to paint the porch. One day as the coach was leaving practice, he grabbed one of his players to help him out. "Hey, kid, come home with me today if you don't mind. I need some help with something." On the way to the coach's house, the coach told the player, "When we get to my house, I want you to paint my wife's porch, okay?"

"All right," said the player. "No problem." As soon as the two arrived at the house, the coach went into the side garage and came back with paint and a brush. "Here you go, Tommy. I really appreciate you doing this, and my wife will, too. Here is a beautiful shade of green she will love. I'll be working in the backyard. Let me know if you need anything."

Thirty minutes later, the player was all finished. "Wow!" exclaimed the coach as the two walked to the front of the house. "Boy, that didn't take very long at all."

"Yeah," said the player, "it didn't take long at all. I think it looks real pretty. And by the way, your wife drives a Mercedes, not a Porsche."

A Funny Moment in Sports*

In the heat of battle, all kinds of funny things happen. Sometimes they are not funny at the time, but later make for grins. For instance, we have all heard about Bobby Knight throwing a chair, but how about Coach Mike Krzyzewski?

In a game during the 2006 season while Duke was playing Virginia. Krzyzewski was upset over Duke's play, and with 3:17 left in the first half, he made his displeasure known to the whole building by picking up a chair and slamming it down. During his press conference, Krzyzewski engaged in a tongue-and-cheek exchange discussing just how mad he was. "In my younger days, I did things that were a lot worse," Krzyzewski said. Then he asked with an innocent look across his face. "I don't know what I did. Did I throw a chair across the floor?" Obviously, a reference to his former boss Bobby Knight throwing a chair in 1985. "I wasn't mad during the Virginia game, and I simply picked up a chair because I didn't like where it was."

Humor

"We were tipping off our plays. Whenever we broke from the huddle, three backs were laughing and one was pale as a ghost."
—John Breen

"He could talk me into eating a ketchup Popsicle."
—Beau Trahan on Mack Brown

"Humility is always one play away."
—Tim Foley

"I retired for health reasons. The alumni got sick of me."
—Frank Howard

"I want players to think as positively as the 85-year-old man who married a 25-year-old woman and bought a five-bedroom house next to the elementary school."
—Charley Pell

"Even if you're on the right track, you'll still get run over if you just sit there."
—Will Rogers

"I am so mixed up I feel like I have one oar in the water. No wonder I keep going in circles."
—Eddie Hill

*The Charlotte News and Observer

Billy Tubbs was the head basketball coach for Oklahoma University. During a game one night in Norman the fans were going nuts yelling and throwing things on the court because they thought the calls were so bad. The referees finally called over Tubbs and said, "Look, coach, you have to settle down these fans. They are out of hand and we will give your team a technical foul if you don't do something." "Okay," said Tubbs. He went over, grabbed the microphone, and said, "Alright, people, I am going to ask you to stop throwing things and screaming at the officials, *no matter how bad they are!*" The place went crazy.

D. Ross Cameron / Zuma Press

Other Motivational Ideas

Coaches do all kinds of things to motivate players. Jim Donnan once drove a steamroller through his team's practice at the University of Georgia. Jackie Sherrill famously castrated a live bull in front of his Mississippi State players. Greg Blache, as defensive coordinator for the Chicago Bears, gave players bullets as rewards for big plays.

A few seasons ago, Jacksonville Jaguars coach Jack Del Rio had players swing an ax at a tree stump in the locker room, so they'd feel the power of his mantra: "Keep chopping wood!" Though punter Chris Hanson badly injured his leg with the ax, the team improved.

Baylor's women's basketball coach Kim Mulkey-Robertson said, "She [referring to Sophia Young] makes me look good. She has lived up to the hype and scored 33 points and added 12 rebounds on her way to being the all-time Big 12 scoring champion." All any coach can ask is to teach players and let them use their God-given ability to excel. When asked about the scoring title possibility, Sophia Young responded, "I didn't even know about any records until you guys [the media] brought it up." Some athletes have their priorities in order and, of course, coaches help them get things straight.

A Little Violence Goes a Long Way

Baylor University football coach Guy Morriss says motivational tricks work best if a surprise factor is involved. Two seasons ago, when he coached at the University of Kentucky, Coach Morriss ferociously slammed his fist into a locker because his team was down 17–16 at halftime. He broke his right hand, startling his players. "It woke them up, changed their tempo, their attitude," he said. "They'd been so lethargic in the first half." The team scored 21 third-quarter points and won the game, 45–24.

Coach Morriss suggests that managers consider pounding tables to rally their sales forces. But such potentially bone-breaking demonstrations should be used sparingly, and not just because you have only two hands. "You can't make a habit of it," says the coach. "It's got to be at critical times, when you think you need a radical measure."

Pound the Rock

The Tampa Bay Buccaneers keep a 200-pound boulder in their locker room and lug it to away games. Coach Jon Gruden invites players to "pound the rock" to psyche themselves up for the hard work needed to win. (The rock was credited with helping the Bucs win the 2003 Super Bowl.) Be creative, but be careful!

10

Coaches—The Ultimate Motivators

Jamie Squire / Getty Images Sport

The Evolution of Coaching Motivation

For anyone who played high school or college football in the "good ol' days," motivation may have been synonymous with discipline. Many of the coaches had just returned from World War II. Many had been officers in the military, and their approach to coaching football teams was similar to their approach to leading troops into combat. As one coach told his team at the beginning of the season, "I want to hear three things out of you guys: 'Yes sir,' 'No sir,' and 'No excuse, sir.'" His manner and attitude made them believers on the spot. At a Saturday team meeting after one player had been tongue-lashed a full five minutes for missing an assignment, the athlete's head hung below his shoulders as he murmured his quiet response, "No excuse, sir." Another player from that period recalled a coach's promise during a halftime speech when his team was lagging well behind their opponent, "If you boys don't go out there and play the last half, come Monday I'm gonna run you 'til you puke and then run you through it."

In the '60s and '70s—particularly as those players who experienced military discipline from their coaches became coaches themselves—the general approach to coaching motivation began to evolve. In the place of the familiar hardcore discipline was an easier line. "If you guys pay attention and work hard, I'm not going to be too rough on you," one junior college coach announced at a team meeting with the season just around the corner. "If I see any slackers, things won't be as nice—and neither will I."

A decade later, a player who played high school football and ran track at Panhandle High School in Texas recalled, "When the new coaches came in, we noticed they were nicer," he said. "Instead of chewing us out and tearing us down all the time, they were more positive. They worked with us, built us up, gave us confidence, and told us we could win—and we believed them. And that year, my senior year, we had a winning season."

Although disciplinary measures were still required in some instances, more coaches began motivating their teams with slogans, rewards, and recognition. One veteran coach said, "I had a player who got hurt one season, and when he came back, another kid had worked hard to take his place. When the injured athlete didn't get to play as many downs as he expected, he decided not to show up at Saturday's team meeting.

"Later that day, I went to his house, but he refused to talk with me, so I had no other choice, I cut him from the team. Later, as an adult, that same player had a son who wanted to quit his high school football team, and from what I heard, the kid I cut told his son quitting wasn't a good idea. Cutting a kid was the hardest thing I had to do, but I only used that when there was no other choice."

> "A good coach will make his players see what they can be,
> rather than what they are."
>
> —Ara Parseghian

Yet, you also find those coaches who focused on toughening up their athletes. Some used belt lines. Still others resorted to a game called "bull in the ring," an often-used exercise to keep players on their toes while they served as human tackling dummies for the rest of the team. In this exercise, athletes formed a circle with one player in the middle. Then, as the coach called a player's number, he would charge into the ring and hit the person in the middle with all he was worth. Then, another number would be called and the player in the middle had to survive the next hit.

According to one coach, he used "bull in the ring" once as an assistant coach when the head coach directed him to encourage a certain player, who was sabotaging the rest of the team, to quit. After the saboteur had been hit a half-dozen times, he refused to get up and the rest of the players went into the locker room. The "bull in the ring" victim quit the team that day.

As team spirit became important, some coaches began going the extra mile to relate to the current trends. Team meetings became more fun, the locker room was no longer a place of meditation before games, and some coaches began allowing the players' choice of music to be piped through the training and locker rooms. Coaches found, as Bear Bryant learned in his later years of coaching, that the one-size-fits-all motivational technique would never work.

School rules and rules in athletics were also evolving. In previous decades, a student who became pregnant was usually required to leave school. At a college-based track meet, one coach explained the differences: "Now, not only do we have to arrange for food and lodging for our athletes, we also have to make babysitting accommodations for our girls who have children. Somebody has to be responsible for the little ones while their mothers run," she explained.

Today, coaches are working hard to build team spirit, to instill pride, and to encourage each player to have confidence in their skills and their preparation. It appears that the days of military discipline, of coaches demanding respect and motivating through fear are gone.

Today's coaches know they have to earn the respect of their teams. Coaches work hard to provide the best possible guidance in developing player skills and understanding of the game, no matter what the sport. In most locker rooms, motivation—for the individual and for the team—has become job one.

> "Inspire and motivate your players with praise. Ten years from now, it won't matter what your record was. What will matter is if your kids love you or hate you."
>
> —Jim Harrick

Credibility and Trust

You are coaching a generation that strives on credibility and trust. At Team Up, we are often asked the question: "How do you motivate players who have an acute attitude of indifference?" They are alluding to players who have some ability and skill but at times act as if they are "too cool for school."

On my vocational journey, I made a brief stop in public education. I served as a tutor in a self-contained high school classroom. My challenge was to help push a class of indifferent students through the public school system. These students could have had their picture next to the definition of the word indifferent. This group of students was in a self-contained classroom because of their common apathy toward the educational process. All of them suffered from poor grades and a penchant for disciplinary referrals. They genuinely believed they were too cool for school. These were the students that drove the other teachers crazy. They were not only tagged as troublemakers: most of them *were* troublemakers.

Many of these students were merely biding their time until the time they could drop out of school. After spending a short time with these students, I realized they fell into two distinct camps: those who actually had learning disabilities and those who didn't. In other words, some students in the class were very capable of doing the work and some were not. Most of these Y'ers came from fractured homes and suffered from a lack of parental encouragement. My goal was not just to tolerate them and push them through the system. My goal was to help each student reach his potential. If that was going to happen, I was going to have to earn their trust and build credibility with them—as is usually the case with Generation Y.

I cared that these students learn and make their grades and graduate. My challenge was getting them to care about the same things I cared about, which is generally the situation in all forms of coaching. We care that the players improve, work hard, learn discipline, and care about the team. The challenge is getting them to care about the same things you care about. If I wanted to get through to these students, I knew I would have to connect with them in a positive way. I would have to build trust with kids who were very guarded when it came to trust. At the same time, I would have to build in them a respect for the student/teacher relationship.

My goal was not to become their buddy, which is a mistake many coaches make. My goal was to connect with them and earn their trust. I was the teacher and they were the students—a line that must never be blurred. If I was going to connect with them, they would have to know I genuinely cared. They would have to come to trust me, and they would have to know I cared about them.

Donuts

Detention is the first line of punishment used in many public schools. If a child is tardy or commits a minor infraction, he is put in detention. Students in my class led the school in detentions. In detention, students come in before school and sit watching the clock, hoping for it to tick faster. Most of the students in my class were perpetually behind in their work. What made it worse is that most of them didn't care. I thought to myself, "How can I get these students to use their detention time to catch up on their work?" Then I got an idea.

Having kids of my own, I know one thing: kids like donuts. Kids like donuts in the morning and pizza in the afternoon. Nutritionists may not like them, but kids do—and Generation Y kids are no different. I got permission from the administrators to hold

©2007 Jupiterimages Corporation

detention in my classroom for my students. The first morning, I brought donuts to share with them. I offered them to the students, who were more than skeptical. In a distrusting manner, one of them asked me, "For real?" Slowly but surely, they ate the donuts. Good news spreads fast. The next morning I brought donuts again, and this time I had my students serving detention, but I also had students show up early who were not serving detention. They heard there were donuts. I shared the donuts with all who came in, until the donuts ran out. The next morning I brought donuts again.

As we ate donuts, I spoke great words of encouragement to them. I never spoke words of judgment against them. I encouraged them to catch up on their work and as they finished assignments, I praised them and told them that I was proud of them. That may sound corny to some of you, but I could tell these were words these students did not hear often in their lives. Soon, I had students voluntarily coming in to catch up on their work. On exam days, I offered to study with the students before school started. I also stopped bringing donuts—except on special occasions.

As the trust level developed, I began to place expectations on them. I let them know I expected them to finish their work and I expected them to show respect. If they were behind on their work, I would tell them I expected them to come in early and catch up. The mornings of an exam I would offer to study with them before school. On the first history exam, we had four otherwise poor performing students make As. You would have thought they had just scored the winning touchdown in the Super Bowl.

These students with improved grades began to exhibit leadership in the class. They let the other students know that being disruptive was not cool. They began to put positive peer pressure on the other students to behave. As the semester rolled on, I only occasionally brought donuts. Yet, they continued to improve in both their grades and their behavior. I had developed expectations of them and I held them accountable for their work and their test scores and they were eager to please. I fully believe the secret of their success was that they now had someone they wanted to please. Again, we believe a coach's greatest tool is understanding that every young person wants to please someone. If that someone is you or someone on your staff, you will be in a position to get the most out of that player.

I would like to say all of the students responded and became better students, but that did not happen. I am not a miracle worker, but with most kids from Generation Y, it does not take a miracle. It only takes someone who cares. Making an effort to show you care will not guarantee a positive result. If they think you do not care, they most assuredly will not respond to you. If they trust you, they will play for you.

Growing up, my coaches would have never thought about treating us to donuts and pizza. It would have made them appear soft. They were not interested in connecting with us. They were tough on us and we responded. They were "old school" before it was old. I am an old-school guy, you may be an old-school coach—but these are not old-school times.

Keeping Yourself Motivated Can Be the Toughest Task of All

> "Most people go to work. I get to coach"
> —Jim Valvano

It is amazing how many things can suck the life force out of you when you are trying to do good and simply help people. The hardest thing of all is when you can't quit, you can't fire back exactly what you are thinking, and you just have to smile and take whatever comes your way. Even as a professional, a role model, and a mature human being, there can be days when it is difficult to stay positive.

A wife went into the bedroom one morning to wake up her husband because it was time to go to church. "Okay," she said. "It's time to get up and put on your good clothes. Roll out of bed. It's time to get going."

"I don't want to go," her husband protested. "I don't like it down at the church. The sermons are too long, they're always asking for money, and the people are mean. I don't like them and they don't like me. No, I don't want to go and get rolled over."

"I know," the wife sympathized. "But you have to go. You're the preacher." Many days we feel like that preacher, but what motivates us to carry on? It's true that coaches don't go into the profession for the money. The real reason, of course, is to change lives. While that "higher calling" should be motivation enough, remember the following when thinking about why you coach:

- A coach helped mold your character, and now it's your turn.
- It's actually more fun to teach someone else to make a basket than you making it yourself. Two people get to smile.
- Nothing is like being in the battle when your heart is pumping almost through your chest and you can't wait to see what happens next.
- An incredible play that you dreamed up, that you designed in the dirt with your finger develops right before your very eyes—and it's executed perfectly.
- Players will come up to you in the grocery store years later and say what an incredibly positive difference you made in their life—and you can barely remember their name because you coached so many athletes.
- You really don't care who gets the credit.
- You may be the only true "role model" some players have in this world.
- You coach and keep going with your players because you know life is hard and they might as well learn that now.

> "There are days it's really been fun, and there are days when it's really been, well, trying."
>
> —Jody Conradt, former head women's basketball coach at the University of Texas

- You're good at it and you leave the players better than when they came to you.
- You would be miserable doing anything else.

In the course of writing this book, we talked to many former coaches. Many of them remembered what a pain some parents can be, the low pay, the need for summer jobs, and many other difficult issues. Yet, every one of them loved what they did, and they especially miss the fellowship with the other coaches, the games. "Oh, the games," they'd say. "When it's going well, there is nothing like it." And what they miss more than anything else is the players who they helped and the ones they never got a chance to meet. You could tell there is a void in their lives, now that they've retired.

How do you keep the fire and the passion going? Remember these suggestions as you work on that inner motivation:

- Have a trusted friend, spouse or partner to talk to when times are tough. As a friend, you have a right to say, "I would like to talk to you about ..." then, unload and unleash. Tell the good and the bad and don't hold back. You'll feel better, and remember to return the favor when they need to talk.

- Go to church. It's often like a filling station for most people. A community of faith will look at you and your family differently, and you can cry out to one who hears your needs. Besides, you can sit in church, and at least for an hour no one will bother you.

- When dealing with people, remember you probably didn't deserve the instant praise after a win nor do you deserve the instant criticism after a loss. Coaches are put on a pedestal by a lot of people, but keep yourself humble. Remember, today's headlines wrap tomorrow's dead fish.

- You are more than your team's record. *Never confuse your worth with your work*. Your self-esteem should not be determined by your last season's record. You would never allow a player to believe his self-worth is tied up in his efficiency on the field or on the court, so no matter how others place their expectations on you, realize you are the same good coach whether you are 3–8 or 8–3.

- Set realistic goals. Bill Parcells' Dallas Cowboys were 8–3 to start the season in 2005–2006. The reporters went nuts and had them going to the Super Bowl. Parcells kept holding them back, saying, "Just wait. The season is not over. We're not in the playoffs yet." Things went south. Coach Parcells wasn't playing a game and the truth was, it wasn't even "coach-speak." He knew what he really had and didn't set himself up. In the end, he was right.

- Relieve stress. Find something outside of sports to take your mind off of everything. Every coach needs a break from the pressure. When you are stressed, chances are two hormones are being interrupted: noradrenalin and dopamine. During stress, these hormones can't function properly and you may experience a profound loss of energy and lack motivation. The other thing that happens is suddenly you don't even enjoy the things you once liked. The good news is that you can do something about stress—by exercising, eating right, and getting more sleep. The two other things you can do to relieve stress are to breathe deeper and realize what you can control and what you can't. Remember: you can't help anyone if you don't take care of yourself.

- Lastly, get a dog. If you can get someone to feed him while you are away. He sure will be happy to see you when you get home.

Mario E. Ruiz / Zuma Press

Epilogue

One of our primary goals in writing this book was to share with you the fact that not all people are motivated in the same ways or by the same things. One size does not fit all coaches must be able to adjust. Some things still hold true: players want to follow leaders, and they want to play the games. Coaches have more of an impact than many parents these days, which is a tremendous responsibility. Nothing is more important or lasting than building character and nothing needed any stronger. Use the suggestions printed. It is amazing how many of the coaches whom we have met want to use the new information or object lessons but for whatever reason don't. Trust yourself and your judgment. You have dedicated your life to young people, which is a noble thing, and you are appreciated more than you will ever know by so many.

Feel free to contact the authors Eddie Hill (eddie@motivatingcoaches.com) and Jim Moore (jim@motivatingcoaches.com). We really enjoy discussing these topics, we are always looking for new ways to motivate, and we are willing to help you with your situation. You can also check out our website at www.motivatingcoaches.com and sign up for our free newsletter.

Do you have a great idea on how to motivate your team, or have you heard of a unique idea? If so, the authors would love to hear from you. As always, we will give credit for the ideas you share.

About the Authors

Eddie Hill has been referred to as the "coach's coach" because he helps those in the coaching community motivate their players and build true teams. Eddie's down-to-earth, practical style has been enjoyed by teams, organizations, and companies such as Wal-Mart, Sears, and Microsoft. In 2005, he was featured on Spike TV's nationally syndicated program, *The Reality of Speed*, leading team building for a Nextel race team before the start of their season.

Eddie is the president of Team Up, Inc., based in Dallas, Texas, which provides training, events, and team-building seminars for groups of all kinds. Eddie enjoys being creative in his speeches, writings, and videos, realizing people may not remember what you say, but they will always remember how you made them feel. He wants all coaches to feel great, realizing all the sacrifices they make to help all kids. Eddie is an avid golfer and volunteer mediator for Tarrant County. He earned his B.A. degree from Barton College in Wilson, North Carolina, and his Masters from Texas Christian University in Fort Worth, Texas. Eddie resides in Dallas, Texas, with his wife Karen, his son Austin, and his daughter Allison.

Dr. Jim Moore brings his enthusiasm and insight to *The Coaches' Motivational Playbook*. As a coach of youth sports, he understands the importance of motivating through hard work, object lessons, and creative education. Jim is the vice president of Team Up, Inc., and speaks at coaching clinics, writes articles, and leads interactive seminars that get results. Jim is an avid golfer, and he graduated from Texas A&M University, Texas Christian University, and he received his doctorate from St. Paul in Kansas City, Missouri. He resides in Rogers, Arkansas, with his wife Carol and their three children: Trey, Hannah, and Campbell.

To receive Team Up, Inc.'s free monthly newsletter, which has coaches' interviews, motivational tips that work, and other helpful information for coaches, go to www.motivatingcoaches.com or call 972-896-2179.